People and Cities

STEPHEN VERNEY

People and Cities

with contributions by

COLIN BUCHANAN

RICHARD HARE

CONSTANTINE DOXIADIS

RICHARD HAUSER

RAYMOND PANIKKAR

Fleming H. Revell Company
Old Tappan, New Jersey

SBN 8007-0437-1

Library of Congress Catalog Number: 73-146865

Printed in the United States of America

For

ROBIN, RACHEL,

HELEN *and* KATHARINE,

who will live in the cities of tomorrow.

Contents

CONTENTS

People and Cities

PART I

Happening

Three kinds of souls, three prayers

I am a bow in your hands, Lord. Draw me, lest I rot.

Do not overdraw me, Lord. I shall break.

Overdraw me, Lord, and who cares if I break!

(prayers by Nikos Kazantzakis, quoted by Dr Doxiadis at the beginning of the opening lecture on 'People and Cities')

In the modern city, hate between rich and poor, rulers and ruled, is much easier to preach than love; but unless love is both preached and most skilfully practised, our cities will fall apart.

(a postscript written by Professor Hare after the 'People and Cities' conference)

1. Origins

'I SUPPOSE', said the Bishop, 'that we should invite the Archbishop to preach.'

It was the summer of 1965—way back in the dark ages—and we were sitting in the Chapter House of Coventry Cathedral, wondering what to do to celebrate the jubilee of our diocese in 1968. How does a church celebrate a jubilee? Presumably there would be a great service, with processions and banners and trumpets—and of course a sermon.

We sat for a moment relishing the prospect—outwardly loyal, inwardly bored—and then Simon Phipps, our Chaplain to Industry, said, 'Couldn't we do something for somebody else?'

The story which sprang out of that question, and which will be told in the first part of this book, is about one of the most urgent problems now confronting the human race. It will be told on two levels—of story and autobiography—describing both something which happened, and also the development that went on in my own mind as I was involved in that happening. On the first level, the story tells how men and women from thirty-three countries and during the space of three years explored together the problem of what is happening to *people*, as all over the world they crowd into bigger and bigger cities. On the second level, the autobiography describes how one confused priest had his mind forced open so that he began to understand something about the modern city, and about the role of the Christian community in it.

This book is for other confused people who feel puzzled and concerned about the city, but who don't quite know why. Story and autobiography are often the best means of communicating an idea, because we find it easier to fcllow a story than to grapple with a textbook, and we enjoy going on a mental voyage of discovery with a fellow human being. But there are some ideas, lying deep at the heart of human life, which *can* only be communicated through story and autobiography, as we share each other's first-hand experience, and open up to each other ourselves and our mistakes. It is such an idea, lying at the heart of the modern city, which this book hopes to uncover and to communicate.

'Couldn't we do something for somebody else?' Yes, but what? Our minds began ranging over the great issues of today: war and peace, poverty and plenty, racial tension, and it was decided that Simon Phipps and I should go to London and see if amongst these huge problems there was any immediate concern to which we might offer our little resources. In London, as we talked with men and women in touch with international thinking and development, one word began to emerge—the city. From all over the world there were coming not just rumbles of discontent, but sharper cries of impending disaster, as people from the countryside, the veld, the jungle, the desert, poured into the great unplanned modern cities, and were engulfed in a way of life which threatened to depersonalize them. Perhaps here was a problem which we in Coventry, a compact little city at the heart of industrial England, could at least begin to think about?

The more we thought about it, the more clearly did it emerge that Coventry might be the ideal meeting point to discuss the modern city. The industrial revolution had started in Britain, so we in this country had made more mistakes, and had more experience, than anybody else, which we could now share with other people. Coventry exemplified this world-wide problem, but was itself of manageable size. Our population had jumped from 50,000 to 330,000 since the beginning of the century. We had a booming motor-car industry which continued to attract immigrants. In 1940 we had been destroyed in the first 'blitz' of the war, and this had given our planners the opportunity to build a new city, and to try out new concepts in the design of the city centre and of the peripheral housing estates. Our local council had not been afraid to think boldly and imaginatively, and amongst many other social experiments had pioneered a form of 'comprehensive' education—indeed cynics would say, 'If you want to get something out of the City Council, tell them it's never been tried before'. For like all good patriots, they saw and understood the truth that their city was the centre of the universe—a truth which, as we have known since the days of Copernicus, is in fact true of every place, and to grasp hold of it is of great benefit to mankind at all times, for it opens up the springs of confidence and initiative. The danger, of course, from which our city fathers were not wholly free, is to lose one's sense of humour, and to forget that every other place is also the centre of the universe.

At the heart of the city stood the cathedral. Here again, the old cathedral had been destroyed in 1940, and after the war a new cathedral had been built alongside the ruins of the old. Under the inspiration of its former provost, Dick Howard, it had been designed as a powerful symbol of Christian forgiveness, of death and resurrection; and now under the creative leadership of its present provost, Bill Williams, it had become the centre for a new pattern of team ministry, out of which was emerging a new vision of the role of the church in the modern city. As in the city, so in the cathedral, we knew that we had something worth sharing with the rest of the world, though we too lived and worked under the ever-present danger of taking ourselves too seriously.

There was a third factor which made Coventry an ideal centre to study the modern city. Around the city lay the County of Warwickshire, containing a number of smaller towns and some two hundred villages set in fertile and beautiful countryside. The life of these villages was changing drastically. After twenty years of agricultural revolution the farm labourer was ceasing to exist, and his place was being taken by the tractor and the combine harvester. Men and women from the villages now went to work in factories, and well-to-do city people were building themselves houses in the villages to escape from the ugliness and the hurry of city life. More and more the towns and the city encroached on the countryside, as children were drawn to them for their education, teenagers for their recreation, housewives for their shopping. And this attraction of the city was setting up its own tensions, for two worlds with two different ways of life were coming into collision—the city with its vigorous, hopeful, thrusting ways, and the countryside with its courtesy, its wisdom, and its sense of community.

I myself had experienced this collision in a most dramatic and personal manner, and at a profound level. I was born in a village, and spent the impressionable years of childhood in a countryside where rooks cawed in elm tree tops and primroses carpeted the woods, and from a medieval church tower the bells rang out on Sunday morning over the fields—there were three bells, and they called out urgently, 'Come to church, come to church,' and then for the last minute one little bell took over, telling you to hurry up because the service was just going to start. Most important of all, every person in the village was immensely significant—Mr Carter the big game-keeper with his leather gaiters, Miss Coleman the little old lady in the alms-houses—and we belonged together. My family had lived there for 450 years, and so probably had theirs, to judge by the names on the gravestones and in the records.

It was therefore something of a contrast when my first job as a priest took me, after the war, on to a new housing estate which was being built near Nottingham. Here I saw trees being cut down, and thousand-year-old top-soil being bulldozed up. Whole streets were built at a time—first the drains, then the foundations; next wooden frames were set up into which concrete was poured; and when the frames were taken away, there were the walls and doors and windows of a row of houses. The roofs were put on by a crane, the electricians, plumbers and painters followed each other in rapid succession up the street, and at the end of the process came the furniture van, depositing a new family into each new home. When these young couples arrived they thought they had en-tered paradise, for they had been for five years on a wait-ing list, and this involved living either with mother-in-law, or in rooms where the landlady would bang on the wall if the children made a noise. But after six months their happiness had too often given way to loneliness, and sometimes to hysteria. I remember one young mother who told me she felt so dreadful that she was tempted to throw her baby into the River Trent. 'Come over the road,' I said, 'and I will introduce you to another young mother.' So we went across and told the story to her neighbour, who looked at me pathetically and said, 'I feel just the same myself.' They felt that they didn't belong, and that nobody knew them or cared whether they lived or died. It was paradise lost.

As I now understand, looking back, we were involved in a very bad bit of planning. In fact Nottingham at that time had no planning officer, and the city architect and engineer were doing a good job according to their lights, housing a great number of people in a short time at the minimum of expense. When I arrived, some 2,000 people were living there, and when I left six years later there were over 20,000, but the result was an aesthetic and social desert. All the houses were the same height and the same shape, most of them were concrete, and they were all Council-owned. I remember the district midwife resigning her post after being there about eighteen months, and saying to me, 'I shall go crazy if I have to go into another house that looks exactly the same.' The City Council seemed to think that this uniformity was a virtue, and forced it upon us with paternalistic authority. For example, every one of the 6,000 houses had to have a privet hedge. I myself planted a beech hedge, and when the Parks Department tried to root it up I told their workmen that I had informed the City Architect about it in person (this was true. I had mentioned it to him at some reception). This apparent alliance between the church and the architect preserved my beech hedge for three years, at the end of which time I moved house, leaving the sturdy and beautiful little hedge to my successor. Within a few days it had been torn up, and a scraggy little one-year-old privet hedge planted in its place.

But there were more serious defects than this. No playgrounds were provided for children, though every house was inhabited by a young married couple, and where the occasional lawn had been planted there was a notice, 'Keep off the grass.' There were no community buildings, so that if any group wanted to meet for any social purpose —for example, to run a dance—they had to use the school hall, where a 'No Smoking' notice frowned down on them, and they were at the mercy of the caretaker who agreed only as a personal favour to open up his territory after school hours.

There were many other mistakes made, which fifteen years later we can recognize as belonging to the bad old days of planning, but probably the worst mistakes of all were made by me, the parish priest. I was so horrified by the ugliness, the loneliness, the suffocating paternalism, that I wrote off the City Council in my mind as wicked men, and openly attacked them. By so doing I destroyed the only hope of making things better. Being young and exasperated, I vented my frustration on the politicians and the city officers, not observing in my immaturity that they were just as puzzled and anxious as I was, and that my role should not have been to castigate and alienate them but to draw them into discussion, to win their confidence, and to find a solution together. Through this first mistake I was led into a second, which was to promote the church as a separate social organization, and to be jealously fostering a kind of ecclesiastical empire over against the secular. This again was done for the best of reasons, because in fact only Christian organizations survived in that desert. All the others fell out with each other and their initiatives collapsed, whereas we apparently held within our community some secret of compassion and tolerance which enabled us to persevere. We set up meeting points for those lonely young mothers, organizations for the children, and, as the community grew, youth fellowships and clubs for the over-sixties—it was at this point that I first began to understand the marvellous power of love to build community in the modern city. But what I did not yet understand was that if the Christian church is to be the true midwife who helps a community to be born, then it has to give up the search for power and prestige and help other people to become their real selves in their own way. This is true not only of the church, but of all who are trying to serve and build a community. As a sociologist has said,[1] 'You can try to get the credit for social change, or you can get social change. You cannot have both.'

Those years in the housing estate were the most formative in my life, for I had the privilege of entering for the first time into the experience of city people. A parish priest meets people at their most personal, at moments of acute happiness and unhappiness, and as he is involved with them and prays for them over the years he comes to know them very deeply in all their strength and weakness. What struck a country-man most forcibly was that we were a society without roots, and this made us insecure. We were even more insecure because we were at the mercy of great industrial economic forces beyond our control, and the chief topic of conversation was our work and rates of pay, and whether we might do better to move to this or that company. But I began to see that there were advantages in not having roots. For instance, vegetables have roots, and animals have not, but animals can go places. So amongst my city friends I encountered a boldness to experiment, a readiness to embark on the unknown and to tackle the impossible, provided always that we would do it together and give each other some encouragement and strength. I also learnt from them what the church really is: not a medieval building—we had no building for several years, but we worshipped in a builders' canteen where the winter wind blew through the cracks in the walls, and the rats ate the heart out of the harmonium— but a company of people who are open to each other, who have been grasped by a certain truth, and who have a common purpose.

My next move was to a village in rural Warwickshire,

[1] Robert Theolbold, *An alternative future for America.*

where the population given in the local register was 350, the same as it had been in the Domesday Book compiled some 900 years earlier. Here I found myself back in a natural community where everybody knew everybody else, where they were connected by a marriage network, and where they looked after one another in times of need. The quality and pace of life were totally different from those on the housing estate, and it was difficult to believe that one was living in the same century and in the same country. For example, on the housing estate I could visit five or six people in an hour, having a friendly word with each and passing on. In the village it was insulting to leave the house in less than half an hour. We were persons meeting each other in a courteous and unhurried manner, exchanging news, and discussing the affairs of the village. I remember how, soon after our arrival, my wife and I went to supper with a farmer and his family at about 9 p.m., and some three hours later we stood up to leave. 'But you haven't seen round yet', said our host, and he took us on a midnight tour of his stables and showed us his prize-winning cattle.

If the last six years on the housing estate had been the most formative years of my life, the next six years in the village were the happiest. It is fashionable for sociologists and anthropologists to decry village life, and to insist that we should not be romantic and nostalgic about it. Certainly it is true that village people lived in great squalor before the industrial revolution, and that their communities were often inbred and socially ossified. The village idiot was a reality, and so was village gossip. Even in my village in the 1960s we knew too much about each other, and the whole community vibrated with any little tension or scandal. But, if we are searching in this story for the secret of community, then let it be said quite bluntly that a modern village is a more humane community than a modern city, by which I mean that people have more room to be themselves, and that on the whole they care more about each other. It is nonsense today to think of the country clodhopper whose only conversation is 'Eh! ah!' With cars and television, it is becoming more and more true that country people can enjoy the sophistication of the city without its noise, ugliness and pollution. With the new wave of commuters building their homes in the country, the village community is becoming varied and very rich in its texture, while remaining small enough to be conscious of its identity. Of course the new elements do not always mix with the old, and the village is divided into factions— the townees and the villagers, or the sherry drinkers and the tea drinkers—but if these tensions can be accepted as creative, then the modern village within reach of the modern city is probably the best setting for a happy life that has ever been available to the human race in all its million years of history.

In the village I came back to the old truth that individual people are of ultimate value, and I saw how each one can grow and develop when he has room to express himself, and when he lives within a framework that gives him security. There was no juvenile delinquency in our village, and the boys and girls grew up full of initiative.

I began to see also the strength and the weakness of tradition, and what sort of roots we should and should not have. If tradition ties us to the ways our fathers did things then we are like vegetables which have roots and cannot move. For example, I remember the Church Council proposing that the kerbstones round the graves in our churchyard should be taken up, so that we could use the comparatively new invention of the motor-scythe to cut the grass. This led to an outburst of indignation, and a charge of sacrilege (we were disturbing the resting place of ancestors' bones). But if, on the other hand, tradition makes available to us the wisdom of our fathers while leaving us free to react and adapt to the pressures of our own generation, then we are not vegetables but 'radicals'. A radical is literally (from the Latin *radix*, a root) 'one who goes back to the roots of things'. The word has come to mean 'those who hold the most advanced views of political reform on democratic lines' (*Oxford Dictionary*). A radical is thus a realist, because he understands and distinguishes two important facts, first that human nature does not change, and second that environment does. The human nature of Odysseus or King David (1000 B.C.) is not different from our own to any perceptible degree, but the environment has in the meantime changed almost out of recognition from that of ancient Ithaca or Jerusalem, and in the last fifty years it has been changing with increasing speed. A realist in our day will therefore hold conservative views about our human nature, and 'advanced views of political reform on democratic lines' about our institutions. If we could grasp this distinction, we should already have cleared away a lot of confusion in our discussion of 'People and Cities'.

We should also have hit upon the most important clue in our investigation into the role of the church in the modern city. In our village of less than 400 people the old parish system worked beautifully. The vicar could know everybody, pray for each family every week, and organize a network of care for their needs. The old parish church stood in the centre of the village, the embodiment of its history, and the symbol of an unchanging love that guarded over it. Here week by week its joys and sorrows, hopes and anxieties, could be lifted up in prayers and psalms and hymns, and if our voices were not always in tune, at least we belonged to one another, and shared the same concerns together, and so our worship was real.

But during those years which we passed so happily in the village it was becoming obvious to anyone with eyes to see that the old system was breaking down in the city, where a vicar was often required to look after 10,000 or 15,000 people. The people were the same, but the environment had changed, and the institution needed to be overhauled by 'political reform on democratic lines'. So, reluctantly, in the autumn of 1964 and six months before this story begins, I had returned to the city.

From village to city, back to the village, and into the city again—the effect was like that of a Turkish bath, where you go from the hot steam into the cold water, back into the steam, and out again into the water. This violent juxtaposition of experiences wakes you and shakes you up and puts your senses on the alert. So it was that when in the summer of 1965 it was decided that part of our jubilee celebrations in 1968 might be an international meeting to discuss the modern city, and when I was asked to head up the preparations for it, I already knew in my bones that this was one of the crucial issues of the twentieth century. I had no clear intellectual grasp of the problem— but as I discovered in the next three years, there are very few people in the world who have.

2. Focus

'COULDN'T WE do something for somebody else?' That question asked in 1965 seems now to be oddly out of date, and alien to our present way of thinking. At the time it marked an advance, for it was coaxing an introverted church to turn outwards and away from its obsessive concern with building up its own life, and to get on with serving real human needs. So far so good—but does the form of the question conceal a patronizing innuendo, and does it still belong to the passing age of paternalism? Perhaps I ought only to speak for myself, but I certainly imagined that our conference would be the occasion for the 'developed' countries to pass on a lot of information to the 'underdeveloped' countries—I imagined grateful people coming to Coventry and being given a lot of 'know-how', and going back to build a happier Asia, Africa or South America. This gave me a very warm and comfortable glow of inner satisfaction, tempered by a little disquiet that I didn't myself know the 'know-how'—but I supposed that somebody else did. One of the delightful achievements of our conference which took place three years later was the shattering of this complacement and paternalistic attitude, for the contributions made there by Asians, Africans and South Americans were outstanding for their freshness, their vigour and their penetration, and it became clear that we were all 'developing' together—though none of us knew exactly towards what. But this is to anticipate.

As a first step towards launching our project we invited a representative body of fifty Coventry citizens to meet and consult together one Sunday afternoon. The invitations went out over the joint signatures of the Mayor and the Bishop, and the company which assembled in the medieval Guild Hall included the following: the Town Clerk, and the Vice-Chancellor of the University; six members of the City Council; the City Planner and his deputy; the Director of Education and the Children's Officer; a headmaster and two headmistresses; three doctors, one of whom was a psychiatrist and another a paediatrician; executives from local industry and commerce, and two trade union officials; the Chief Constable and his deputy; bank managers, lawyers, clergy, college lecturers, architects, civil servants and social workers; representatives from the world of art, sport and the working men's clubs; a justice of the peace; and, finally, a housewife. As they took their seats, one sensed a significance about this meeting that was over and above the content of its discussion. What did it signify, what did it point to, this gathering of so many different professions to think together about the city—this bishop, on a Sunday afternoon, presiding in a city hall over a discussion on urbanization?

Three speakers had come to open up the subject for us. The first two were a geographer and a sociologist, and their different approaches complemented each other most happily. Sir Dudley Stamp, the geographer, described the background to the modern city and urged us to accept the 'city region' as the new social reality, while Professor John Mays, the sociologist, focused our attention on the city itself, and within the city on the key issue of 'community'. By the time we broke up for supper they had enlarged our thinking about the contemporary world, and disturbed many of our previous conclusions. Here are some of the ideas which they presented, and others which they provoked.

The fact of overriding importance today is, of course, the population explosion. The world population will have doubled by the end of the century—the increase is now 65 million people in one year, or the population of a sizeable city every day—and the rate of increase is accelerating as the knowledge and practice of birth control outstrips the knowledge and practice of birth control.

This explosion of population is alarming enough in itself when we consider the extra mouths to be fed in a world where half the people are already hungry. But its consequences are seen to be even more alarming and explosive when we discover that this rapid growth is concentrated in the cities. In fact the rural population of the world is static or even declining, while everywhere ancient cities expand and new cities spring up, and the result is a cataclysmic change overtaking the human way of life. After a million years or so during which we have been primarily hunters and peasants, we are now approaching the moment when we become preponderantly city dwellers—the world balance will tip in about 1970, and during the next century cities are likely to grow to ten times their present size.

In Britain we are already well past this half-way mark —it is now probably true to say that 90 per cent of our population lives in towns and only 10 per cent in the country—and we are already experiencing this change in the way we live. Our agriculture, which was for so long a way of life based on the rhythms of nature, has passed through a revolution and is fast becoming an industry, organized on business lines to produce food for hungry townspeople. This revolution has brought enormous advantages. Machines now enable us to plough and reap with far less hazard from climatic conditions. Chemicals enable us to control both weeds and animal diseases. The geneticist, the plant and animal breeder, can produce new strains and increase production. But all these innovations have made their most drastic impact upon the farming community itself, which has already dwindled to $3\frac{1}{2}$ per cent of the population, and continues to decrease. The farm labourer who remains has become a modern technician, who must be both a tractor driver and a vet in a white coat.

As the individual adapts to new techniques, do our social structures adapt to the new demographic pattern? British history provides an intriguing case study of this problem. About 1,500 years ago the Anglo-Saxons invaded this island, and being agriculturalists they chose the most fertile land, and established their farms, hamlets and villages. Little market towns emerged as trading centres for these villages, and King Alfred (who burnt the cakes worrying about these and kindred problems) divided his kingdom up into counties, with their county towns. This is the basic social structure of Britain, with its origins in the dark ages, and surviving into the present day.

It was the church which gave it a more definite local shape through a system of ecclesiastical parishes. The old pagan lord of the land appears to have had the duty of providing worship for the community, which duty he had delegated to a priest. He himself continued to provide the place of worship, from the receipts of which he expected to make a profit, while the priest became his agent for conducting the worship, and was rewarded by certain property rights—he was allotted twice as much land as an ordinary member of the village—but these rights also involved him in certain duties, such as providing a bull and boar to service the animals of his neighbours. After the conversion to Christianity, this partnership of landlord and priest was carried over into the new religion and was consolidated into the parish, which had over the years to be accurately defined for the collection of tithes. After the Norman invasion, this whole system was literally 'petrified' by the building of churches in stone, and these beautiful parish churches with their dog-tooth Norman arches, their soaring early English columns, their decorated windows and perpendicular fan-vaulting, are now one of the glories of England—enshrining and entombing her history. But they are at the same time one of the bulwarks holding up reform, for they perpetuate a social system which has largely passed away.

The first major change came 200 years ago with the industrial revolution. As coalfields were developed, a new pattern emerged, with cities growing up in relation to these coalfields and built round factories. Britain became a palimpsest, that is, two patterns superimposed the one upon the other. Today neither of these patterns makes sense as they are administered independently, for the county is deprived of its industrial focus where so many of its cultural activities are concentrated, and the city is deprived of its agricultural zone, where so many of its workers sleep, and on which all its citizens depend for their recreation.

There is a new reality emerging, which is the synthesis of these two and which is expressed by the concept of the 'city region'. Not only in Britain but increasingly throughout the world, this is the concept we must learn and adopt, and according to which we must govern ourselves, because this is in fact the social pattern in which we are all interdependent. Within this city region the city centre will have to undertake certain obligations towards the whole area. For example, is it right that the 10 per cent who live in the countryside should have to keep it tidy at their own expense for the 90 per cent who live in the towns? There is a growing resentment amongst the farmers towards the city slicker who comes and leaves his rubbish for somebody else to clear up. Should the farmer be paid not only for his produce, but also for his labour in keeping the countryside open for recreation?

Such questions may seem to be peripheral, in more senses than one, when we turn to the city at the centre of the region, where the 90 per cent are crowded together. For here we discover that civilized life for the human race is itself in danger.

As this story unfolds the reader will gather that I have an over-all optimism about the city. But nobody has the right to be an optimist until he has some idea of the catastrophe towards which we are now racing, and perhaps at this stage the most vivid way to see it would be through the eyes of those scientists who have been studying animal behaviour. Dr Edward Hall, in his book *The Hidden Dimension*, describes the effect of overcrowding on rats. 'Normally rats have a stable social organization, with accepted rules about property, courtship, mating and the rearing of families, but under the pressure of overcrowding these rules broke down. Females lost their housekeeping ability, and the young—scattered at birth—seldom survived. Gangs of hyperactive males invaded private burrows, trampled the young and sexually assaulted both males and females. Other males turned passive, avoided both fighting and sex, and huddled quietly in corners like catatonic schizophrenics. The colonies, rent by virtually every form of perversion and pathology, teetered on the brink of collapse.'[1] Dr Hall believes that this is caused by overstimulation leading to a state of *chronic alarm*, and that overcrowding amongst human beings produces equally traumatic effects. 'The

[1] From a review of Dr Hall's book by John Kord Lagemann in *Readers Digest*, September 1968.

implosion of population into cities is creating "behavioural sinks" potentially more lethal than the hydrogen bomb. If the problems of such ghettos are not solved, they may well make cities uninhabitable.' This judgement does not seem exaggerated when we look at the slums of Calcutta or São Paulo, when we read reports of increasing violence from cities everywhere, and when we think once again about the forecast of population growth—a world population doubled, and cities ten times their present size. (I suggested above that the consequences of this growth might be alarming and explosive, and the words were chosen carefully.)

To meet this threat we are developing the new science of city planning. The 'first-aid' objective of the city planner today must be to prevent chaos and breakdown, whether the problem is human overcrowding, traffic congestion or the pollution of air and water. But has he a more positive role? As the work of a doctor is not only to heal sickness but also to promote health, has the city planner the function of promoting the health of the community?

This word 'community' points to the key issue—how can people live *together* in the modern city, and so develop their full humanity? Community implies relationships with each other, some common goals, some responsible group action. Is it possible for the planner to influence these intangible things? Can he so design a neighbourhood that he encourages this interaction of the people who live in it while at the same time preserving their necessary privacy? Do some environments positively promote mental health while others actually harm it? My own observations on the housing estate where people felt isolated, and Dr Hill's more dramatic experiments with overcrowded rats, would suggest that bad environment does cause mental ill-health; but some sociologists claim, on the strength of accurate surveys, that this is greatly exaggerated, and that people bring their own mental health with them—for example schizophrenics and drug addicts tend to congregate in twilight zones. Whether or not the planner *can* promote community, there is further disagreement as to whether he should even *try* to do so. Let him obviate the obvious scandals! But do not let him attempt to force people into sociability like Big Brother in a holiday camp, for though people like to interact some of the time, they also value solitude. A man who had lived for seven years in a New York flat was recently moving out, when his neighbour whom he had never seen before opened his door and said, 'Gee, I'm sorry you're leaving. You've been such a good neighbour.' The good neighbour in the city may be somebody who minds his own business and makes no noise—most of the time. But there is another story from New York which shows the opposite danger. A young girl was murdered outside her own apartment, and though the murder was in full view and took some time to complete, thirty-eight of the local residents failed either to come to her aid, or even to lift the telephone and ring the police. Such may be the frightening consequences of keeping myself to myself.

One aspect of community which the planners could deliberately foster is family life. The family is a resilient institution which adapts itself to all conditions, but it deserves a home where thought has been given to the needs of its different members. For example, we are discovering the folly of housing a mother with little children in a twentieth-floor flat. Half the population of a Western city today is under twenty-five years old (in less prosperous continents the figure may be nineteen), but we seem to forget this and to cater largely for the middle-aged—and their motor-cars. Children need streets which are free from traffic. They need adventure playgrounds where they can grow up happily without becoming too docile—dirty, big playgrounds full of junk, where their imaginations can run riot.

Another problem is that of mixed communities. Do we want to encourage people of different classes, incomes and races to live cheek by jowl? It would seem, in the short run, to be easier and happier to live separately in our different ethnic groups and our class-conscious suburbs, where there is less strife and less democracy. But in the long run these 'ghettos' have a tendency to explode or stagnate—and in any case, what sort of human society are we aiming at?

This question brings us finally to politics. It should not surprise us if politics turns out to be the focus of our inquiry and the key to the development of the city, for the Greek word *polis* means city, and 'politics' is the science of the city—or rather the science and the art of governing (steering) the city so that it *becomes* what it really *is*. And what, really, is it? What sort of governing creates the true city? During the last thirty years 'Government' has become more centralized, and this is inevitable in an age when motorways cut across local authorities, and a computer does the arithmetic of ten thousand clerks. But as a result the individual feels more and more that he counts for less—he may at any moment be declared redundant—he is at the mercy of the tycoon. So he drifts into apathy. He opts out of politics. He thinks cynically that anyone engaged in public affairs is either a crank or a man on the make. The heart of the political problem at the heart of the modern city is how to encourage the individual, in this age of centralized government, to believe in himself and to participate in the governing and the creating of his own community.

By the end of the second speech we had absorbed as much wisdom as the mind could take in one afternoon. After supper our third speaker, Lord Holford, the city planner, announced that he was going to show us some slides. We sat back and enjoyed some visual aid, while he showed us what his colleagues had talked about—great cities in every continent, some of them planned, others of them not; some soaring into the air, others sprawling over the countryside; some beautiful, others hideous—and as we looked we understood most vividly that this is the new habitat for the human race, and that our concern must be with *people* as all over the world they crowd into bigger and bigger *cities*.

Moved by this concern, a member of our city council, Peter Lister, proposed, and the company agreed unanimously, that we go ahead and hold a world conference.

3. Insight

THE GATHERING of citizens described in the last chapter
had seemed even more important than the question it was
discussing. It seemed to point to something beyond itself
or to signify something hidden within itself. During the
next few weeks I came to understand what this was.

Two questions were continually in my mind at that
time, 'What is the city?' and 'What is the role of the
church in the city?' The more I studied the city, the more
I was struck by its complexity. There is the variety of
its buildings—homes, offices and factories, hospitals,
schools and churches; theatres and art galleries; restaur-
ants and pubs; shops, law courts, libraries, swimming
baths, banks, hotels—all of which are criss-crossed with
a variety of networks—roads, railways, telephones, gas
and electricity, water and drainage systems—and the
whole is serviced and kept in order and in motion by an
almost incalculable variety of trades and professions—
Architects and Butchers, Chemists and Draughtsmen,
Engineers and Funeral directors, Grocers, Hairdressers,
Ironmongers, Journalists, Key cutters, Launderers, Musi-
cians, Newsagents, Opticians, Plumbers, Quantity sur-
veyors, Removal contractors, Solicitors, Tailors, Uphols-
terers, Vets, Welders, X-ray operators, Youth-workers and
Zoo-keepers, to mention but a few of them. Within all this
exuberant variety and complexity of the city, what is the
role of the church, and what is the particular function of
the priest or minister? We will concentrate here on the role

of service to the community—not forgetting that there is another role which may be described as wonder, insight, adoration, worship.

In past ages the church was often a pioneer of social services—as though it had some sensitive antennae which picked up the peculiar needs of each generation before they were generally recognized. At the time of the collapse of Rome, St Benedict founded his monasteries which became centres of education. The church continued to be the only provider of education through the dark ages and the middle ages, and the chief agent of education right into our own century, when it has gradually been taken over by the state. Similarly with medicine—the church provided the original hospitals. In days when rivers flooded every year and travelling was dangerous, the church built bridges. Today these services are rendered by secular bodies, whose titles still have about them a curiously religious ring—the Ministry of Health, the Ministry of Transport. In the villages, church alms-houses were the first homes for old people; in the cities that grew up during the last century, much of the neighbourhood life centred on the church hall, and an organization such as the Boys Brigade was founded as 'an extension of Christ's kingdom among boys'. At the centre of this web of charity was the parish priest.

Today these same needs are being met by a host of secular public servants, some paid, some voluntary. Welfare departments care for the old people, and can provide material help on a scale which is quite impossible for the church. For example, a single cripple may be given a hoist to lift him out of bed, a rail to carry him downstairs, and a mechanical chair to take him to work—all of this costing thousands of pounds. The probation service looks after ex-prisoners, and marriage-guidance counsellors advise on matrimonial problems—and if these counsellors get ten matrimonial problems brought to them for every one which is taken to the clergy, it is because people recognize that they are better trained and qualified in this field. The social life of an area is no longer centred on the church but on community centres, working men's clubs, youth clubs, folk groups and a multiplicity of societies which keep tropical fish or fly carrier pigeons or sing Gilbert and Sullivan operas.

What is the parish priest to think about all this? As he watches the advance of secularization does he, as one young priest put it to me, suffer from an 'Elijah complex'? 'I have been very jealous for the Lord God of Hosts', said Elijah to God, 'because the children of Israel have forsaken thy covenant, thrown down thine altars, and slain thy prophets with the sword, and I, even I only am left, and they seek my life to take it away.' But the Lord replies, Tut, tut, Elijah. Open your eyes and look. Go and anoint the secular authorities whom I have chosen to carry out my purpose—'Yet I have left me seven thousand ... which have not bowed unto Baal.' So the parish priest today, as he opens his eyes, sees that the causes of yesterday have triumphed, and that the love which he is commissioned to represent is now in fact operating through thousands of colleagues.

Has the church, then, any longer a specialist social service which it can render? This is where the antennae have to reach out, and we have to ask ourselves, 'What is the peculiar need of society in our day?' The answer is staring us in the face, so close that we do not see it. *The peculiar need of society today is for people to meet each other*—not only neighbours across the street, but also specialists across their professional boundaries.

This arises directly out of the complexity of the city. We are all specialists, and no one of us can understand the whole. Many different and highly skilled professionals must co-operate to promote the well-being of the city, or even of one individual in it. Unless we communicate and co-operate, our complex cities cannot function. Unless we integrate ourselves, our cities will disintegrate.

Here is the specialist social service which the church must pioneer at this moment of history. It has no monopoly of it, and in a few years' time some other organization may have taken over, and the church will once again move on. Already, because this *is* the social need of the moment, sensitive people in every profession are aware of it—schools of 'urbanology' at the universities are linking together various faculties concerned with the city, and the Seebohm Report is urging that the social services in Britain should be unified—but there are still walls of suspicion to be broken down everywhere, and deep chasms of prejudice to be bridged between people who misunderstand each other because they speak the same words but not the same language. These are the bridges which at this moment of history the church is uniquely qualified to build—for three reasons. First, because it is ubiquitous—its members penetrate most nations, most cities and most situations. Secondly, because it is (or should be) neutral, as between races or professions, and can offer a meeting point where people generally can be open with each other. Thirdly, because this bridge-building is its original work, as laid upon it by its founder. The word 'complexity' is derived from the Latin *complector,* which means 'I embrace', and the complexity of the modern city is an opportunity for people to embrace each other in a great variety of human relations. If the church has any skills, any techniques, any experience worth anything at all, then they are in this realm of loving one another.

Here one must add that the church is uniquely *not* qualified for this role. A few years ago, in the new steel

town of Durgapur in India, different Christian denominations approached the Hindu development officer, Mr
Sivaramakrishnan, and asked for sites to build their separate churches. 'Gentlemen,' he replied, 'my problem is to
unite this city. Come back when you have the answer to
the problem, and are not a part of it.' Yet in spite of its
failings this remains the church's role, and as we shall see
later this has been most signally demonstrated in Durgapur
itself.

At the beginning of this chapter I mentioned the two
questions which were pressing on my mind during 1965;
the first, 'What is the city?' and the second, 'What is the
role of the church in the city?' It was a dawning percep-
tion that the provisional answer to my second question is
'to help people meet each other', which led me to stumble
upon an equally provisional answer to the first.

One day I got talking with our senior probation officer,
and we discovered that we liked each other. We also discovered that we had many aims in common, and that our
work dovetailed. So we began having lunch together, and
it then seemed natural that we should each invite a
couple of friends to join in our conversations. Thus, there
came into being a little company of six, comprised of
another probation officer, a children's officer, a planner
and a lecturer in social studies. We met once a month
for lunch, with no formality or agenda, but simply because we enjoyed it. The discussion never failed to fas-
cinate, and the group is still in existence three years later,
including three of its founder members—the other three
having left the city. It now meets in the evening so as to
give time for more relaxed conversation.

I have described this little company because I believe it
is typical of the kind of church which is emerging all over
the world. As we talked we opened each others' minds,
communicated a lot of information, and became an actual

fellowship of people in the city who could co-operate easily on a basis of trust. One thing which the others clarified for me was the function of the priest over against that of the social worker. During the last decade many priests and ministers, exasperated with an out-of-date system, have resigned their posts to become social workers, but what the social workers themselves need most is not one more colleague so much as a minister who will really minister to them. I discovered this one day when the two probation officers and I happened to be having lunch without the others, and in this more intimate company the conversation turned to prayer. Then they told me of the utter exhaustion to which their work sometimes brought them, and their sense of impotence in face of the problems which overwhelmed them. At such a moment they needed somebody to go to—they who seemed so strong and capable to their clients—somebody who would listen and encourage, and say a prayer for them and give them a blessing. They needed a person of compassion, but also of authority, through whom they might make contact with the peace which passes all understanding.

As the year went on, we decided to gather a few more friends, and to spend a week-end together at William Temple College, Rugby. This college was founded in memory of the great Archbishop who had thought so deeply and spoken so forcibly about the social issues of the 1930s and 1940s, and it is a place of research and of training for Christian social work. So it seemed a suitable venue for some twenty-five of us to go and think together about the question, 'What is the city?' Our discussion was opened on the first evening by the prophetess who was at that time the college principal, Mollie Batten, who puffed at her pipe and uttered her oracular wisdom through clouds of smoke like Apollo's priestess at Delphi. The next day a planner, a social worker and a minister described their jobs, and then as we talked together the miracle happened once again—the barriers fell between us, and we became one in our search for the common goal. Perhaps the most profound moment was when David Driver, the Methodist minister, described his work as prison chaplain in Manchester, and how one afternoon he had come out after some difficult interviews, with all the great questions pounding in his head, and wondering whether after all there was any such thing as redemption—whether men really could start again—whether there was any purpose or sense in his work. His honesty and his doubts spoke more deeply to all of us than any success story could have done; and the next morning, which was Sunday, it seemed perfectly natural that most of us should receive the Holy Communion together (though I had never even asked those invited whether they were Christians), and the breaking and the giving of the bread seemed to sum up and express what was between us. So we went home, and a few days later I was thinking to myself that we had never answered the question, 'What is the city?'—when all at once I saw that we had. And this is the answer. As we open ourselves to each other and to the truth, as we seek together to build the city—WE ARE THE CITY. The goal is already in the process. We are the thing we are looking for.

4. Outlook

IT WAS these two insights about the city and the church which now guided our preparations for the conference. We decided to approach selected people in cities round the world and to invite them to set up 'workshops'—in each city the convener or host would be 'the church', and the workshop would be a small group drawn from different professions. Thus the preparation would be as significant as the conference itself, for in each place we would initiate a fermentation, and the goal would be already present in the process.

On another and more practical level, we hoped by this system of workshops to gather first-hand experience out of a number of different situations, and so to penetrate beyond platitudes and into the heart of the world problem. We would wait till the reports had been received and collated and only then would we decide, three months before it started, what the conference would be about.

This programme worked itself out over the next two years very much as planned, except that in most of the cities the fermentation did not have to be initiated. It was already happening. We discovered this through the World Council of Churches.

The visitor to Geneva may be bewildered when he is referred to the Advisory Group on Urban and Industrial Mission in the Division of World Mission and Evangelism of the World Council of Churches. But if he perseveres he will find, camouflaged by this monstrous title, a little cell of revolutionaries. They are seven in number, drawn from Zambia, India, Argentina, Germany, Japan, the U.S.A. and Britain, and with a secretary in Geneva. Their members—some clergy, some laity—are all involved in social work, and they include a bishop and a professor of social ethics.

I had first contacted the secretary of this group, Dr Paul Löffler, during 1965, and he had told me of an increasing number of Christian centres round the world where radical thinkers—most of them still suspect by the institutional church—were pioneering experiments in 'industrial mission' or 'urban mission'. This did not mean going into factories or shopping centres and preaching to the workers during the lunch hour, but rather listening and learning, trying to understand the intricate problems of industry or the city, and making friends with the people concerned. It took different shapes—an academy in Germany, a single worker-priest in Japan—but in general it was based on what is called the 'new theology', and on the theory not so much of taking God into the factory as of finding him already at work there, not so much of getting people into church as of co-operating with them in advancing the kingdom of God through the development of the secular city. During the winter of 1965 Paul Löffler had sent a circular letter to all these centres, in which he wrote, 'As I see it, the time is now ripe to compare notes between such experiments in different parts of the world, to evaluate some of the first tentative findings, to test the assumptions and presuppositions which are made.' Later in the same letter he wrote, 'Urban planning represents another crucial issue . . . How can Christians and churches participate in it . . . how can we bring about a dialogue with the city planner and the sociologist?'

So, immediately the project of a conference had been launched and accepted in Coventry, we wrote to Paul

Löffler and his chairman offering them this meeting point for the exchange of ideas, and asking for their help in contacting people round the world who might set up workshops in preparation for it. They agreed most readily, and sent us the names and addresses of some sixty people to whom we posted an outline of our plan. About half of these replied, offering to convene workshops in Johannesburg, Kitwe, Accra, Melbourne, Osaka, Taejon, Calcutta, Durgapur, Madras, São Paulo, Buenos Aires, Los Angeles, Chicago, Boston, Helsinki, Prague, East Berlin, Mainz-Kastel, Glasgow, Liverpool, Swansea, Cardiff, Sheffield and Nottingham—there were others in the league who subsequently fell out. We also set up three workshops in Coventry City to represent the city centre, a suburb and a housing estate, and nine in the county of Warwickshire representing the towns and villages. So the framework of a world-wide inquiry was constructed.

In July 1966 the Advisory Group was to meet in Switzerland at a little Alpine village near Geneva, and they invited me to come over and discuss the conference with them. The express train out of Geneva took me to a lakeside junction, from which a mountain railway wound up through the meadows and into the pine forests and deposited me in mid-afternoon at St Cergue. As there was no meeting till later, I walked up through the forest and out into a clearing where a little grey-headed man in a polo-neck sweater—or was it a faun?—sat leaning against a tree, gnarled like the roots, and with a sense of hidden vitality. It turned out to be the Bishop of Middleton contemplating the panorama of Alpine peaks all of which he had climbed over the years—or Ted Wickham, as he is more familiarly known, one of the original and most courageous pioneers of industrial mission, and now the Chairman of the Advisory Group. He took me down and introduced me to his colleagues. They included

Masao Takenaka, a professor of Social Ethics from Japan where the Christian church numbers only a half of one per cent of the population, and Reverend John Wagner from Los Angeles, who told me of a project he was starting together with his city planner—they were inviting the people of that vast city to participate in defining their own goals, and so in determining the development of their own city.

As this remarkable group of men talked together, I learnt how urban and industrial mission was gathering strength round the world. They reported on two regional meetings which had recently taken place—one for Africa at Lagos, where fifty church leaders both lay and clerical had attended a training course; and another for East Asia at Kyoto, Japan, where sixteen countries had been represented and had discussed common strategy and the contribution of the church to politics. Two more such regional meetings would take place shortly—for Europe at Bad Boll in Germany, and for Latin America at Buenos Aires.

Our project was discussed and, after some hesitation, accepted. The opposition centred on the question of money, and was led not by a member of the group, but by an observer who was a church bureaucrat from the United States. We took an instant dislike to each other. When I began to expound our plan, he cut me short and demanded to know where the money was to come from. This had me at a disadvantage for we had so far given it very little thought, and I had come to St Cergue prepared to discuss the idea but not the financing of it. Exasperated by my woolliness he dominated the meeting, pressed his attack, and ended with a scornful prognostication that in the end I would come cap in hand, as so many others had done before, and expect the American churches to bail me out. The next day I discovered that this bureaucrat was leaving on the same train as myself, and during the journey we had the opportunity to talk to each other as two human beings. Before we got to Geneva I had grown very fond of him—he was really only a big overgrown boy like the rest of us. He had, however, put his finger on our weakest point, and he was quite right in his pessimistic prediction; we did go cap in hand to the American churches—but they gave us nothing, and in the end my own optimistic conviction was vindicated that if the idea was good enough someone would back it.

I returned to England chastened by this encounter, but even more humbled by the recognition of a great world-wide movement in which we might be able to play some tiny part, an onslaught breaking down old patterns of thought, a power as of evolution itself flowing like a river through human affairs and directing men into new associations. Our work would not initiate anything, any more than the grape initiates the ferment which turns it into wine, or the child initiates the river in which he swims. But we could offer at least a clearing house for information, or at best, if certain incalculable factors operated, a meeting point where people from different races and professions could become together the thing they were looking for.

The international framework was now built, but it was still only a framework—a skeleton which had to be filled with life. Paradoxically, this framework or skeleton had been built by the holy church, but was now quickened into life by a secular builder, Dr Constantine Doxiadis.

I met Dr Doxiadis in Athens a few weeks later, at a moment when I felt thoroughly bewildered by the complexity of the subject, and full of anxiety because we now had a system of workshops but we couldn't define the questions to ask them. I was like Ezekiel, when he saw in a vision the valley full of bones. But the Spirit of the Lord spoke to him, and showed him first how to bring the bones together, 'there was a noise, and behold a shaking, and the bones came together, bone to his bone', and then how to breathe life into them, 'and they lived, and stood up upon their feet, an exceeding great army'. The same experience now happened to me; and in my case the Spirit spoke through Constantine Doxiadis—but this should not seem at all astonishing to any one with any experience of who the Spirit is and of how he operates.

I had had my first contact with this remarkable personality some months before, when one evening my wife burst into my study and said, 'You must come and listen to this programme. There's some Greek talking about city planning.' Rather unwillingly I came, and listened to a voice speaking almost perfect English but with a delightful foreign accent, and with that extra quality of enchantment which comes when a man is utterly convinced that what he is saying is true. He was describing a city of the future which wound across the countryside like a huge and undulating spine. It was divided into small neighbourhoods which were intimate and free from traffic, so that children could play safely. A fast motorway or monorail ran down the centre of the spine, so that people could move swiftly to any part of the city, and the countryside was within easy walking distance for everybody. What impressed me most of all was the concern this speaker obviously had for people, his insistence on 'the human scale' in planning, and his optimism that in spite of the inevitable growth of cities we *could* build a humane environment if only we started now to think accurately and to act bravely. So I immediately wrote and asked if I might visit him on a forthcoming visit to Athens.

'Some Greek' he certainly is, brave in war, shrewd in politics—hospitable, ambitious, a philosopher[1]—above

[1] The three Greek words are *philoxenos, philotimos, philosophos.*

all a man of action. He has been a soldier, a resistance fighter, a cabinet minister and a university lecturer, he has written books, founded a new discipline called 'Ekistics' and been decorated by four countries. But by trade, as he himself says, he is a builder—in which capacity he has received the Aspen award as the most distinguished planner of our day. 'Some Greek' indeed, a descendant of Odysseus, always restless and travelling; some Greek, too, I thought, because he didn't answer my letter. Greeks don't clutter themselves up with engagements as we do in the West, but keep room for spontaneity because in their wisdom they know that life without spontaneity is death. So when I got to Athens I played the game according to the Greek rules, rang the Centre of Ekistics and asked if I could meet Dr Doxiadis now, this morning. Yes, came the answer. So I went round, and was shown into the Director's room, and there in the middle of a busy day he gave this unknown foreigner half an hour of his time. For me that half hour was like an experience of conversion.

We discussed the plan for the international conference, and then I asked him, 'Do you think this is worth doing? Will it help?' 'That all depends', he said, 'on whether you and the other participants are clear what questions you are really asking. If you aren't clear, then you will only increase the confusion. There are many possible questions you *might* be asking.' He then picked up a pen, and began to draw the following diagram on a quarto sheet of paper which I still have in my possession.

'The city', he said, as he wrote the column of words on the left' has five components:

1. Nature (air, soil, water, etc.)
2. Man (body, senses, mind, etc.)
3. Society (the family, community, etc.)

4. Shells (rooms, cars, buildings, etc.)
5. Networks (transportation, power, communication, etc.)

	Economic	Social	Political	Technical	Cultural
Nature					
Man					
Society					
Shells					
Networks					

'Each of these components,' he continued, as he wrote the words along the top, 'or the city as a whole, can be looked at from five points of view:

a. Economic
b. Social
c. Political
d. Technical
e. Cultural.'

He then drew in the lines, and asked innocently, 'So how many questions are there to be asked about the city?' 'Twenty-five', I hazarded. I had fallen neatly into his trap. 'Thirty-six million', he declared triumphantly, scribbling the figures along the bottom of the diagram.

He then proceeded to show me by drawing crosses on the grid how an apparently simple question might have many different interpretations. I cannot remember the examples he took, but here is one which will serve. The question is frequently asked, 'What is the effect of the city on family life?' One person might answer this in terms of higher rents to be paid for homes (4a). Another might think of wider educational facilities available to children (2e). Another might emphasize the effect of shift work on the family life (2a, 3d); another, the difficulty of courting couples getting across a city to meet each other, and when they meet of finding somewhere to sit. (This question of making love seems to cover the grid with crosses. It involves nature, man, society, shells and networks and has economic, social, technical and cultural aspects—everything, that is to say, except politics. But in the end politics is 'making love', steering the city towards its consummation when people communicate and co-operate and embrace each other in a perfect complexity. Love and politics are the whole system!)

'But the grid in its present form', continued Dr. Doxiadis, 'is still far too simple, because, when we use the word city, one person may be speaking of a little city of 50 thousand inhabitants, and another of a great conurbation like London with over 10 million. We must divide the city into units of city life, or we will have the greatest possible confusion. It would be like speaking of an army company and a group of armies as similar phenomena.' So he proceeded to set out fifteen units of community on an ascending scale, beginning with the home and the street, and rising through the neighbourhood, town, city, metropolis and conurbation to end in 'ecumenopolis', the city of the twenty-first century when all our present cities will have extended their tentacles and met in an international network.[2]

'The grid which we must now draw of the city will be three-dimensional, and the questions to be asked about the city will now run into billions and trillions. Have you decided which of these it is that you want to ask?'

As he talked I could almost hear it happening, 'There was a noise, and behold a shaking, and the bones came together, bone to his bone.' I had known all these things

[2] See *Between Dystopia and Entopia* by C. A. Doxiadis (1966), p. 55.

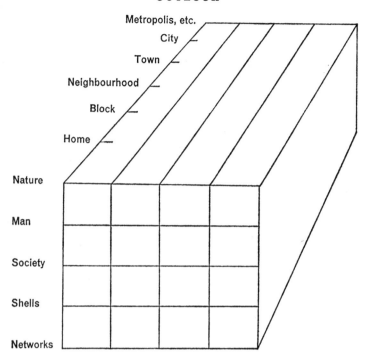

Metropolis, etc.
City
Town
Neighbourhood
Block
Home

Nature
Man
Society
Shells
Networks

Economic   Social   Political   Technical   Cultural

before, separately and confusedly, but now they were forming themselves into a system which the mind could grasp. The word 'ekistics' means the science of human settlements, and what Dr Doxiadis was doing at the Centre of Ekistics was curiously similar to that which I had seen as the role of the church—he was bringing together specialists with their separate insights and allowing them to interact on each other and to build the city together. As I walked home through the hot streets of Athens and the glare of the noonday sun, I felt quite light-headed, but it was not from sunstroke. My first lesson in ekistics had been one of these rare 'moments of truth', when the pupil and the teacher coincide. A difficult decision still lay ahead, as to what questions we should send round the world, but now in my own mind the bare bones of the city were at least becoming an articulated skeleton, to lay alongside that other skeleton which was our international framework of workshops.

That autumn in Coventry a group of us wrestled with the definition of the questions. Following the pattern of the ekistic grid, we invited an economist, a sociologist, a local-government officer, a planner and a minister of religion to submit a list of key questions about the city, each from his own point of view. We also set up groups of 'ordinary' people, the planned rather than the planners, to throw up more spontaneous reactions. A mass of interesting material came in—but it had no life, there was no breath in it. It would not be an exciting adventure for people in Australia or Latin America to answer strings of questions, however apposite they might be. We wrote to Dr Doxiadis again, asking him to advise us how to shape all this up into a syllabus of study. There was no answer. He was travelling. His secretary wrote diplomatically. We responded more and more frantically. 'The date for sending out the syllabus has passed ... The impetus will flag.'

Then, literally out of the clouds, the voice spoke. From an aeroplane over the Atlantic Dr Doxiadis wrote a very humble letter which I quote unvarnished. 'I apologize for the delay in my answer, but I had to take more time to think how I can help for the study of such a complex problem.' He went on to define the subject matter, and continued:

With such definitions accepted we turn our attention to the most difficult problem of all: how to classify the material we are concerned with. I think the most useful way for us to proceed is to move in the following order:

A. Subject
B. Problems
C. Attitudes
D. Goals
E. Solutions
F. Implementation.

In the first two chapters (A and B) we define our subject in order to avoid confusion (this is the greatest
danger), and then we clarify the probems we are
facing. If we achieve this, we have already done something very important.

In the second two chapters (C and D) we clarify our
attitudes (are we observers of evolution or active members of the process?), and only then can we get on to
the goals of the city; otherwise our goals may be confused.

In the last two chapters (E and F) we then proceed to
conceive desirable solutions and to think how we can
implement them—who, how far, etc.

He then set out the three dimensions of the ekistic grid
which I have already described, and drafted at some
length a syllabus of study which sorted out our questions
into appropriate sections. He ended with this postscript.

Conclusion: I am in favour of a consistent questionnaire that is going to force the participants to think of
what they have, and take a position as to whether it
is good or bad (B), define their attitude (C), force thinking about goals (my God, why do we forget them?)
(D), lead to thinking about solutions—entopias[3]—(E),
and how we are going to build them (F).

[3] 'What we need is a place where the dream can meet with reality, the
place which can satisfy the dreamer, be accepted by the scientist,
and some day be built by the builder, the city which will be in-place
—the *entopia*.' Op. cit. Introduction p. XIX.

Better few questions but clarified (B, C, D, E, F) than many but not clarified.

Why cry and not also propose? Or why dream and propose, without defining what happens around us?

I hope that I am clear!

C. A. D.

This advice brought our material to life. The bones stood up and became an army. Within a few weeks a booklet had been posted to our workshops round the world which was not so much a syllabus of study as an incitement to evolution. Our strings of questions were pushed aside into appendices, so that the main guts of the inquiry would show up stark naked; and under the headings which had been suggested to us we wrote as follows (I extract the key phrases):

A. *Subject*. We begin with a simple presupposition —that human beings need human relationships to be fully themselves.

B. *Problems and Opportunities*. We pose a simple question as the basis of our study. How do people meet, and to what extent do they care for one another, in a modern city?

C. *Attitudes*. Accurate observation is valuable in itself, but is it enough? To what extent (a) does your society as a whole (b) do you as a group seek to influence the affairs of your city? To what extent is this possible? Do religious considerations affect your attitude?

D. *Goals*. What are we aiming at? What sort of a city? What quality of life for people?

E. *Possible Plans*. How can we so organize the modern city, that people may more readily meet and care for each other?

F. *Implementation.*

(1) What proposals for action in your own city arise out of this study?

(2) What are your priorities for action?

(3) What would you like to see discussed at the conference 'People and Cities' in Coventry, June 1968?

(4) What is the relation between prayer (as understood by each member of your group) and implementation?

5. Travels I

MANY PEOPLE warned us that an international discussion on 'People and Cities' would be so complicated as to be almost impossible. 'Your delegates will come from different cultures and different stages of economic development,' they said. 'They will not have common problems, and they will use the same words with different meanings. "Democracy" means one thing in Western Europe and another in Eastern Europe. The "housing problem" in Nairobi is how to get some sort of temporary roof over the heads of immigrants—in Glasgow, how to demolish the solid slums and re-house people in sophisticated suburbs.' The trillions of questions that might be asked about the city would be further confused by a babel of tongues.

During the autumn of 1966, while we were waiting for the Workshop Reports, some generous friends in Chicago offered to pay my travel fare round the world as a fee for three lectures which I would give them on the way home. So in January 1967 I started out on my travels. Puck promised King Oberon to 'put a girdle round about the earth in forty minutes' and to search for a little flower that would bring his master the secret love, a flower that had been struck by Cupid's fiery shaft,

> *Before milk-white; now purple, with love's wound,*
> *And maidens call it love-in-idleness.*

The best I could hope to do, with the help of jet planes, was to girdle the earth in forty days; and though in fact

I was in search of that same flower, I phrased it rather differently. I set out with two questions in my mind:

1. Is there a common problem at the heart of every modern city?

2. What is the new shape of the church that is emerging in cities all over the world?

ROME

I stayed only twenty-four hours in Rome, so there was no opportunity to examine the first question. But the second was being debated everywhere. Rome is the centre of a vast ecclesiastical structure, and the most heavily 'over-churched' of any city on earth. Its churches are museums of exquisite cultural value, or rather mausoleums which no longer express the living spirit, while the Castle of Saint Angelo positively typifies the perversion of the gospel. It is a fortress where the pope could take refuge and be defended by an army, and a special escape route to this castle was built from the Vatican—a great wall with an interior passage along which he could flee when attacked by rebels or heretics. Through the holiness of Pope John, the Spirit seemed to have escaped out of these structures and to be blowing about in all the rooms, offices and hotels where I talked to people. 'After Pope John, we begin to breathe', a Jesuit Father said to me. Another Jesuit, who celebrated the Mass in English for my benefit, talked during breakfast about this problem of the church's over-heavy organization. 'We must have a structure', he said, 'but it should be organism, not organization—something living that brings people together. If organization stops people communicating, then it has gone wrong.'

In the Secretariat for Unity I asked Father Stransky about the Roman Catholic Church's attitude to the urban revolution. He told me that there had been a beginning of interest after the war, with the publication of *Revolution in a City Parish* in France. But the rest of the world said, 'This is a peculiarly French problem, and you can't talk with the French anyway.' Now a new interest is emerging, but it is based on financial poverty rather than on theology. 'We are asking ourselves, "Are our buildings too expensive? Should we use the money for other things? Do they make us too bourgeois?" and not the theological questions which are raised in Protestant circles.' (He did not appear to be pulling my leg as he said this, and it made me feel somewhat hypocritical.) One of the great opportunities of today, Father Stransky thought, was the foreign community that lives in every city. For example, there are 1,700,000 U.S. citizens living abroad; they are on the whole intelligent, rich and educated—but they mostly live in ghettos. Equally there are Asians and Africans in Europe, often highly intelligent people who may stay for a few years, and move on. What contribution can these people make, and how can they help to build up a world outlook? (I was to meet this question again in Asia.)

The main purpose of my visit to Rome was to meet Dr Raymond Panikkar. Two years earlier, in setting out the proposals for a conference, we had suggested, 'There should probably be a theologian to address the full conference near the beginning and a saint or prophet, if such a one can be found, to address it near the end.' In the meantime I had met Raymond Panikkar—and had promptly invited him to address the conference in the middle.

To describe this man in terms of his race or profession would be irrelevant, for he is uniquely himself. That he is half Indian and half Spanish, or that he lives half the year over a Hindu temple in Benares and the other half at Harvard University, or that he is a Roman Catholic

priest who lectures in philosophy in six languages, these
scraps of information about him are otiose. We were to
meet for dinner at the Hotel Sporting to discuss the part
he would play at Coventry, and Dr Panikkar arrived a
little late and rather exhausted, for he had been all day at
a philosophical conference, and had been chairman of
a group that spoke in many languages. He embraced me,
and asked me to sit and have an apéritif while he spoke
for ten minutes with a student. This young man, as he
afterwards told me, was on the edge of schizophrenia,
and he seemed to be one of a great number of Romans
and others who were seeking out Raymond for 'pastoral
care'. As we sat at dinner, and in his room afterwards, he
was called to the telephone five times, and was answering
in fluent Italian, German and French. 'What can I do?'
he said. 'They demand miracles of me all the time. I can
only encourage them—speak for a moment—and pass
on.' He would leave Rome the next day on a non-stop tour
via Germany, Scandinavia and Britain to the United
States, lecturing everywhere and holding seminars, shocking, mystifying, delighting, with his conviction that at the
heart of things is perfect joy.

ATHENS

I visited Kosta Mitsotakis, who had been my friend and
agent in the Cretan resistance in 1944. During the last
few years he had become virtually the ruler of Greece, as
Minister for Co-ordination in two successive governments. The door of his bedroom now bore the marks of the
rifle-butts which had smashed it in during the night of 21
April 1967, when Greece had been 'set free' by the present
Junta. Kosta had been held for some weeks in custody,
and then under house arrest; at the time I saw him he was
free to move about, but both he and his family were constantly followed. As we sat together in a *taverna* the waiter

came up and whispered, 'you are being observed'; a secret-policeman was at the table next to us, leaning back to catch our conversation, and when we got up to walk home he followed us.

Kosta and I talked about democracy—the first of many talks on this subject which I was to have on my travels. He spoke from his experience as a cabinet minister, and insisted that what we wanted was more democracy and not less. 'It's easy to say, "Democracy doesn't work. The people can't understand the issues, and won't vote for the necessary cures, so we'll set up some form of dictatorship." But this doesn't work either—you *cannot* impose on people, because they just won't co-operate willingly and so the policy won't succeed.' So first, he said, we need more education and more communication—giving people a chance to assess and trust their government. But at the same time we need more efficiency, with more power given to the government and less to parliament. 'Parliament must preserve its ultimate right of veto, and the general election must give the final word to the people, but probably the House of Deputies should be smaller, so that we have fewer and better men, who have more prestige and are less dependent on their supporters.'

It is impossible to pronounce a verdict over this issue of the Greek military coup that declares one side to be 'guilty' and the other 'not guilty'. Democracy in Greece had sunk into an appalling state of degeneracy, where bribery was rife amongst politicians, even the law courts had ceased to command respect, and every morning the newspapers screamed their daily ration of irresponsible slander from crisis headlines. The army have restored some stability, and cleared up some corruption. But they have done it at the expense of freedom. The press is muzzled. Not only army officers but policemen, civil servants, local councillors, school teachers, have been removed from their posts

and replaced by the nominees of the Junta. One democratic liberty goes, the apparatus of the police state inevitably takes its place.

Kosta escaped in August 1968, crossing to Turkey in a
little boat, wearing a false moustache.

Meanwhile, what of the church? Paradoxically, the
Orthodox Church is outwardly the most conservative institution on earth, yet at the same time it holds within itself the most revolutionary doctrine about 'heaven', which
could be, and should be, the inspiration of today's radical movement in urban and industrial mission.

Outwardly, the age-old liturgy is performed, un-
changed for 1,500 years, speaking of a pure joy and an
ultimate compassion which is beyond the vicissitudes of
history. The icons of Jesus and the saints continue to stand
as transparent windows into an eternal reality. 'Come to
church,' they seem to say. 'Lift up your hearts, and with
the cherubim and all the company of heaven cry, Holy,
Holy, Holy is the Lord.' Yet at the same time they are saying something else: 'We are symbols representing a universal truth. Everything is in a sense transparent, so that
you can see God within it. Look at the world around you
and give thanks, and you will see that everything is holy.'
Here is the contribution which the Orthodox Church can
make to the busy, activist West, and to the secular Christianity of our generation. We are learning that *everything*
is holy. They know that everything is *holy*.

As yet there are few signs that the Greek church is alive
to the urban revolution, and this is not surprising, because Greece consists mainly of villages and small towns.
But for those who have eyes to see, it is now one great city
region round Athens, and part of a European industrial
complex which is draining away its country people into
the factories of Germany. One remarkable bishop has
acted upon this insight—Eirenaios of Kastelli, a little

rural diocese in western Crete. Here on the outskirts of the city region is one of the outstanding examples of urban mission in the world today. Bishop Eirenaios has sold the gold ornaments of his church to build technical schools where the boys and girls from the villages can learn trades and crafts. He has set up an experimental farm to demonstrate new agricultural methods, and to improve the quality of animals and crops. He holds local conferences where farmers can learn how to organize co-operatives— and how to keep accounts so that they can trust each other. At the heart of this work is a new academy, opened in 1968, 'to help the church in the dialogue with the modern world, to encourage the ecumenical encounter, to promote the social integration and economic development of the country'. Significantly, in his own church Bishop Eireanaios has removed the iconostasis (the icon screen) that stood between the people and the altar. There is no more need of peep-holes into heaven. As we were told nineteen centuries ago, 'There will be no saying "Look, here it is!" or "There it is!"; for in fact the kingdom of God is among you—within you.'[1] Transfigured by the Spirit, *everything* is *holy*.

DURGAPUR

Out of the jungle of West Bengal, there has arisen in the last ten years the new city of Durgapur. It consists basically of six company townships, centred upon six industrial enterprises which include one of the largest steel mills in India. Here is to be seen the fantastic change which is coming to the whole of Asia: first-generation industrial workers, who have moved out of an almost unthinkable poverty, live in well-built houses in a garden city, with modern facilities, shopping precincts and recreational clubs. Yet they riot and smash the place up. Why?

[1] Luke 17: 21 (New English Bible).

Mr Sivaramakrishnan, the Chief Executive Officer of Durgapur, believes that the problem at the heart of Durgapur is paternalism. All the company managers want to be ideal employers, and they make available to their workers every kind of facility from cricket to cremation. But it is they, the bosses, who decide what is needed, and the workers feel a deep resentment that they are being looked after. 'All these community centres are concessions', they say, 'to ease the managers' consciences. This is not our place, it's their place.' So they break it up—and the managers retire in dudgeon into the protection of their own club-house. They came to Durgapur to run efficient businesses, not to do this thankless task of community development.

Meanwhile the workers have succeeded in establishing 'our place' in the middle of 'their place'. When Durgapur was originally being planned, it was found necessary to move a number of villagers from the sites allocated for new factories and towns, and they were rehoused along a mud track in a little settlement called Benachitty, with the legal provision that their houses were for residence only. Before long these canny villagers had broken the law *en masse,* and had turned their houses into shops, or pulled them down to make way for markets, cinemas and banks. Now Benachitty has become the commercial centre and the main meeting point of Durgapur. In this beautifully planned area it is totally unplanned. Everybody seems to have installed his own telephone or electricity system, and wires criss-cross in all directions. The road is too narrow. Crowds mill about and the traffic, made up of rickshaws, buses, cars, cyclists, taxis and holy cows, grinds to a standstill at rush hour. But here people are happy. In the other beautifully built markets, so carefully planned, with broad squares and seats in the shade of trees, with rows of symmetrical shops and easy access, there is an almost total silence. Over a given period the comparative trading figures are: in the planned markets of all the townships put together, 7 lakhs of rupees; in Benachitty alone, 37 lakhs of rupees.

Here is the revolt of the human spirit against paternalistic planning. Mr Sivaramakrishnan talked non-stop and very fast for two and a half hours, as with a superb grasp of detail he developed his thesis that somehow the people themselves must participate in the creation of their own city. 'We need more democracy,' he said. Of course there is a danger that democracy may lead to inefficiency, but this brilliant and energetic man would not be prepared to tolerate inefficiency or to sit down under it, like some of his fellow countrymen, and counsel patience. 'In the developing countries', he said, 'urbanization will generally follow the Durgapur pattern and industrial managers will be the main figures in building up the institutions of the new city. So we need training schools where people with experience and foresight can make their know-how available to these managers, and at the same time to government officials, civil servants and trade union leaders.' As a start, he has himself convened in Durgapur a Local Industries Conference, where at least the managers can meet and talk together. 'It is easy enough to bring the managers together,' he said. 'But how about getting them to meet the workers?' Then, turning to Kenyon Wright who was sitting next to me, he said, 'The church is the only banner under which everybody can come together, because you don't threaten anybody.'

Kenyon Wright is a Scotsman and a Methodist minister, who has spent twelve years in India, and by being his natural, humorous, receptive and intelligent self has become part of India, and is accepted as such by Indians. He is Director of the Durgapur Ecumenical Social and Industrial Institute, and in his team at the time of my visit were Reverend Subir Biswas, an Anglican priest; Mr Ramteke, a sociologist who was away studying in Switzerland; Mr Joel Underwood, an American Congregationalist; and Miss Rita Mukerjee, whose grandfather had been a freedom fighter against the British and was known as the Tiger of Bengal. She told me that her grandfather had been in the train one day with a British officer who objected to this Indian sharing his compartment. So when he appeared to be asleep, the Britisher threw his shoes out of the window. Later, the officer went to sleep, and the Tiger threw his jacket out of the window. 'Where is my jacket?' he asked on waking. 'It has gone', said the Tiger, 'to keep company with my shoes.'

Now she and Ken and their colleagues from all nations keep company together, and pioneer in pioneering a Christian experiment which is welcomed by Mr Sivaramakrishnan, the Hindu Chief Executive Officer, as being vital to the health of Durgapur. They have rid themselves of ecclesiastical clutter. They have metaphorically thrown all their jackets and shoes out of the windows, as the first Christian pioneers were told to do—'Provide . . . no pack for the road, no second coat, no shoes.'[2] so the 'church' operates with no church building, with no rotas of sidesmen or deacons, and no appeals for repairs to the roof. Little groups of Christians meet for study, discussion and prayer in the different townships, in the house of one or other of their members, and once a month they come together in the local school for a more formal act of public worship. Meanwhile all the money that can be raised has gone into the Institute, which is there to serve the community.

Rita Mukerjee concentrates on the local needs of Durgapur. She has inherited her grandfather's passion for India, and she believes in democracy—her work is to foster

[2] Matthew 10: 10 (N.E.B.).

a democratic spirit and democratic action amongst ordinary people. She therefore encourages groups, and helps them to become articulate, but she will not organize them. 'Community development', she said, 'is helping people to help themselves. If I do something for them, then this is social work. What I think they want is not necessarily what they do want, and my work is to encourage them to know their needs, and then to do something practical about them. Community is not something you can define—Mr Sivaramakrishnan said to me the other day, "don't ask me to define that word"— but the nearer you get to it the less you want to define it, and the more you want to help people develop it.' But with all her passion for democratic action there was about her a certain Indian tranquillity and dignity. 'In England you never relax,' she said. 'My impression is of people tearing about in a hurry but going nowhere in particular. In India we still have time for people, and for each other.'

Kenyon Wright, together with his immediate work of bringing together the different elements of industrial Durgapur, where twenty languages are spoken, is more and more concerned with a wider field, for the Institute is becoming a training centre for the whole of India. I met there seven students—a chemist, a personnel officer, a Roman Catholic priest and four ministers of various denominations, all of whom were going into full-time work in urban and industrial mission. Through Kenyon Wright's teaching, and even more through his example, they were learning two things: how to enable people to think and act together about the problems and opportunities of modern India, and at the same time how to look at the modern world with the insight of the Bible, and to recognize what God is saying and doing through the events of secular politics.

CALCUTTA

The drive into Calcutta did not show me corpses lying in the streets, as press reports which I had read in England had led me to expect, but vigorous life going on along the pavements, with stalls and street vendors and shoppers moving in a general bustle. As we reached the centre of the city, we saw the old British colonial architecture, with its stately banks and law courts, government buildings and churches. A tour of the city the next day confirmed the impression of a huge commercial centre with its teeming variety—here a Hindu area, with a crowd of gentle friendly men and of stately women in saris; there a Muslim pocket, with its mosques and its street scenes that might have been lifted straight out of the Middle East, with men in turbans sitting and smoking hookahs, looking dignified and rather dangerous. But the memory that dominates all others is of the slum—or 'bustee'—where we got out of the car and walked around. The overwhelming impression was that one was walking in a sort of open sewer. Sewage running down the gutter of the road from which we entered the bustee; privies gaping and stinking at us—one serving many houses—hardly ever emptied by the City Corporation, so that they overflowed; sewage running down the narrow paths between the houses; sewage blocking the path which had become a quivering bog; sewage oozing into the ponds where people apparently washed themselves and their clothes. But I am not speaking the whole truth if I say that the overwhelming impression was of a sewer. Another impression was even stronger and more shocking—of the dignity of man, and his spirit dominating his environment, of children playing happily (one group on a mud patch was playing cricket), and of a strong family life flowering in the squalor of these hovels. The people laughed and welcomed us. The children crowded round to have their photographs taken, and pressed so thickly that I was not able to get the pictures I wanted of the disgusting ordure—I had to take their laughing faces instead.

Not far from the bustee I saw a building site with a huge notice, 'Luxury flats to let'.

Dr Colin Rosser, the chief planner on the Calcutta Metropolitan Planning Organization, told me that 'the real shock of the situation lies not in the slums but in the statistics. The city is falling behind in every kind of facility, and risks a total breakdown.' The population will almost double in twenty years to $12\frac{1}{2}$ million, and this will mean families without homes, children without schools, men without work, the sick without hospitals. There is a growing congestion of traffic and shortage of water. The surrounding land is marshy and unfit for new building. The port is too small for modern ships. The basic jute industry is threatened with competition from man-made fibres. The economy is stagnant, and the budget in deficit. Above all, the city has thirty-three local governments, and this makes it almost impossible to take a grip of the situation or to implement any coherent plan.

'The heart of the problem', said Dr Rosser, 'is to stimulate initiative and hope amongst the population, so that they won't just wait for money which is not forthcoming anyway, but will use their own wit and ingenuity to tackle their own problems.'

He took me into the conference room to meet a dozen of his young Indian colleagues. 'These are people,' he told me before we went in, 'none of whom have a car or ever expect to have a car, and who are working for the future of their country, hoping that one day their grandchildren will reap the benefit.' Planning as they see it in Calcutta is not the business of controlling and tidying up the city, but rather it is planning for action—defining a number of limited advances which can be made if people

will participate, and then drawing together the administrative, legal, financial, social and economic factors into
a plan of action. 'But the plans won't work,' they said,
'unless there is a psychological change, and the people of
the city say "this is *our* plan, and we are going to make
it work". Somehow we must develop a civic sense. We
must open communication between all sectors of the city,
between rich and poor and between the different language groups.' There is no loyalty to the city as such,
because people do not understand what the city is, though
locally Calcutta holds very successful 'poujahs', or fes-
tivals, and these generate local enthusiasm.

I asked them whether they as Hindus could see how
the Christian church could contribute to the life of the
city, but I discovered that to them the Christian church
meant the organization which gives out free milk, so that
the question could only mean, 'How can Christian social
service be better co-ordinated with everyone else's?' So I
asked them instead about Hinduism, and they explained
that in general it has no social activity, but is entirely
individualistic. Its only community buildings are temples
for individual worship. But one of them told me of a movement within Hinduism called the Ramakrishna Mission,
which is developing a variety of voluntary social work,
and he offered to take me to a lecture which was to be
given at the headquarters of the mission that very evening.

Swami Ranganathananda was giving the concluding
lecture of a course that had been going on for six years,
and his theme that night was the dignity of man and the
nature of democracy. Man in his evolution, he said, advances towards freedom, and this freedom comes when
you see the real, the Ahtman, in everything. When you see
each man's Ahtman, what he really is, then you have
found true equality and the basis of democracy. Every
man has dignity, and no work is ordinary. 'Without a

sweeper, cholera breaks out, and society breaks down—as a machine breaks down without one essential nut and bolt.' Respect a man, and he feels elevated. But if you do not respect him, then he is snuffed out. 'To throw money on the ground for the rickshaw-puller to pick up, or to throw food to an untouchable, is a blot on India.' When you see an educated man do such a thing, you understand 'that education may only add a little knowledge to a man's vulgarity'. After the lecture we looked round the mission centre, which contained a 'chapel of unity', where there is a picture of Ramakrishna in the middle with Christ on one side of him and Buddha on the other. The mission has lecture rooms and libraries, and runs courses of further education. We went out through a great court, which was surrounded by rooms for students and visitors from abroad, and where all the paths were lined with enormous dahlias in pots.

What of the Christian church? The Anglican cathedral is Gothic, and looks like Canterbury. The Presbyterian 'kirk' was built in 1814, and is the counterpart of the church by Waterloo station in London. They were designed as garrison chaplaincies for the servants of the Honourable East India Company, but they are an incubus on their descendents today who want to be the servants of modern India. Of the thirty churches in the centre of Calcutta, one at least is choosing the way of death and resurrection —the Methodist church in Sudder Street. This again is a monument to nineteenth-century British Methodism, with a large site and spacious buildings set in a garden, but these Methodists have asked themselves, 'Is it right to hold on to all this valuable land, and to use it in this nineteenth-century manner?' They are thinking in terms of a strategy for the whole church in Calcutta, and have not only agreed to the general thesis of change, but have taken the almost unheard of step of agreeing voluntarily to their own demolition as a contribution towards this general renewal. They have formally resolved 'that No. 16 Sudder Street be demolished,' and a seven- or eight-storey building be put up, of which four floors shall be offered for business investment. Out of the income so gained, they hope to use the other floors for: (a) a staff member for social development; (b) a staff member for industrial-commercial mission; (c) a child-health unit concentrating on malnutrition, where research can be done, and patients can be referred from the 'bustee' clinics. This new project is to be run by a united management drawn from several Christian denominations. It is a swallow heralding an 'Indian Summer'—which, incidentally, is an old nickname for the beautiful weather which ushers in the festival of All Saints.

By the time I left India an answer was already emerging to my first question, 'Is there a common problem at the heart of every modern city?' Highly qualified experts had suggested to me that there was—and it was summed up in the word 'participation'. In Durgapur the *people* were saying, '*Their* plan won't work unless it's *our* plan.' In Calcutta the *planners* were saying, '*Our* plan won't work unless it's *their* plan.' Here, apparently, was the dilemma at the heart of the modern city—and it had been underlined by what I had seen of Pope John's reforms in Rome and of the military régime in Athens—on the one hand there must be participation, initiative and control by the people, while on the other hand there must be planning, firm structures and efficient government.

To state this problem is not in any way to solve it, for how can unskilled people participate in the technical decisions of the planner or the economist? As computers get larger, industrial companies amalgamate, cities become more complex and world economy is knit into a single system—as in fact we move towards that world government which Professor Arnold Toynbee thinks to be already 300 years overdue—how are people to participate in decision making, how are they to initiate ideas and policy, or to control the demonic power of an impersonal bureaucracy? Over the next ten years this dilemma is likely to become far more acute. The search for a new pattern of democracy, which suits the complexity of the city over the whole scale from 'Coronation Street' to 'Ecumenopolis', will be the central issue of politics.

THAILAND

During the following week the answer became clearer to my second question, 'What is the new shape of the church which is emerging in cities all over the world?' I had been invited to a conference in Thailand of the East Asian Council of Churches, on the theme of 'Urban-Industrial Mission', and delegates had come from India, Pakistan, Thailand, Indonesia, Singapore, the Philippines, Hong Kong, Taiwan, Japan, Australia and New Zealand. This was an opportunity to learn at first hand about countries which I should not have time to visit.

We met 30 kilometres south of Bangkok, by the seaside. Here the Red Cross had built a convalescent home, with water gardens and pagodas, flowering shrubs and a clear blue swimming-pool. Our conference met in 'Happy Hall', and the stewards were nurses in crisp white uniforms. Running parallel with our conference was another called 'Laymen Abroad', which was exploring the theme Father Stransky had emphasized to me in Rome—namely that there are now in every country large numbers of resident foreigners. As the 'missionary' disappears it is the layman, who in all probability has come to the country on business, who is now the Christian ambassador. His role must be to break through the conventional image of the 'superior Westerner', or the 'inscrutable Oriental'; he must desire to meet and to understand the people amongst whom he is living, and he must be ready to serve his host country. The people who were talking like this were themselves economists, business men, service men, government officials, teachers, Peace Corps volunteers—men and women from many nations, and it was obvious that they had been waiting for just such a lead as this conference provided, and that as they talked they were generating new vision and enthusiasm.

Our own discussion, on urban-industrial mission, had about it a ring of confident impatience. These men knew they were meeting at a moment of fantastic change, when hundreds of millions of their fellow Asians are struggling out of an immemorial poverty and towards the hope of some tolerable living standard. They were confident, because after ten years of experience new ways of being the church have proved themselves, and are no longer 'experimental'. They were impatient, because the main body of the church still looks on them as eccentric. This meeting at Bangkok, in January 1968, marked a breakthrough when they changed from isolated and diffident pioneers into a united company with goals, leaders and a strategy. They believe that the role of the church in Asia is to be on the frontiers of change—seeing God at work in the change, understanding it and testing it and guiding it, helping to make tensions creative, keeping in mind always the dignity of man and the new community which is emerging and which 'is beyond the boundary lines of family, tribe, language or nation'. They see that their special role is to stand alongside the urban poor, the squatters in the slums, and to give them a voice; to support the trade unions where they are struggling to be free from paternalistic management; to help identify the injustices of the city, such as victimization by landlords and moneylenders, and to take action against them. In situations of extreme need, such as starvation, it may still be right for the church to take direct action, but in general it is better to encourage the citizens to act themselves, and to change the structures which cause the need. 'If I give a man a fish', said Confucius, 'I feed him for one day. If I teach him to fish, I feed him for his lifetime.'

This kind of church is going to need a new structure. One speaker predicted that 'in ten years' time the building-based congregation will no longer be the norm.' Congregations will emerge that are based on a common occupation or a common purpose, like the group of businessmen in Korea who are working for the development of their country. There will be cells, and there will be team ministries, and they will co-operate with other religious bodies, such as Hindus and Buddhists, or with secular bodies which have the same goals.

All this is not a dream for the future. It is happening fast now. So the conference went on in a most business-like manner to work out training schemes, to provide literature, and to plan finance and strategy for the next four years. They ended by appointing one person for each of five Asian regions to keep them all in touch with each other and with secular agencies, and by asking Reverend Harry Daniel to be their full-time secretary. Harry is the tallest Indian I had ever seen, and outstanding also in the qualities which are demanded for leadership today. He has the humility to listen, to encourage and to enable others. He has a clarity of mind which draws together the elements inherent in a situation, and then expresses them in a clear plan of action. But he has something more, he has serenity of spirit—as though he combined within himself the executive and the 'guru' —and that sense of freedom which comes through being actually 'over-mastered' by the truth.

In this he was typical of the Asian Christians whom I met. It seemed to me that the church in Asia was ahead of the church in Europe, in that it was responding much more readily to the demands of the moment. We are so rich in buildings and in traditions that we are pegged down by them, enmeshed, unable to move. They, in their poverty, are more open to each other, they feel more urgently the needs of their neighbours and the necessity for a new kind of church in a changing world, and they are less cocksure of themselves and so more ready to turn to God very simply and naturally in prayer. So while we talk about renewal, the Spirit actually operates through them and gets on with His work. 'How blest are those who know that they are poor; the kingdom of Heaven is theirs.'[3]

[3] Matthew 5: 3 (N.E.B.).

6. Travels II

I arrived in Japan with two hypotheses which needed testing.

One: *'There is a common problem at the heart of every modern city, and it is* participation.'

Two: *'The church which is evolving in cities all over the world is based on small groups, its social work is to help people meet each other, and its prayer is contemplative prayer, or a river of love flowing through it.'*

What I learnt in Japan totally confirmed these two hypotheses. I was in the country only five days, so that my judgement may not be of much value. But during those five days my whole attitude to Japan altered from fear to love as the result of some deep conversations with some remarkable people. I will try and record what they told me and what they showed me.

The Japanese way of life is still paternalistic. When General MacArthur decreed in 1945 that the country should accept democracy, the Japanese bowed and smiled in their courteous fashion, and agreed. But though the legal forms are now democratic, society still operates on the old authoritarian lines.

In industry, for example, a young man who joins a company at the age of eighteen expects to stay there till he is fifty-five, when he will retire with a considerable pension. During those years the company is his Father. It acts towards him with responsibility, which he repays with loyalty. While he is a youth, the company will provide for him a comfortable hostel, and subsidized transport to work. It will arrange outings for him on Sundays, and offer mountain resorts for his holidays. Parents with marriage-able daughters will even send in their names to the dormitory foreman—and after marriage the couple will move into a company house. The young man may feel a little frustrated at first, particularly if he has tasted free-dom at the university, but the wage structure offers him an almost irresistible inducement to loyalty. Wages go up by enormous leaps for length of service, and there is a large bonus paid every six months for good attendance. Thus at eighteen he may be receiving 20 thousand yen a month, with a monthly bonus of 10 thousand while by thirty-eight he is receiving 70 to 80 thousand yen a month, and the bonus has gone up to 40 thousand. At the age of fifty-five he will receive a retirement gift of between 3 and 5 million yen, according to length of service and status. This financial inducement to loyalty is reinforced by public opinion. If a man moves from company to company he is doing something faintly dishonourable, and he loses face. Within the company there is only one union—a company union, as distinct from a trade union of electricians or engineers—so that strikes are rare, for one does not strike against one's Father, and in any case to be absent from work is to lose the bonus.

This system gives to the Japanese worker an almost total security and it results in a highly efficient industry which can deliver goods to the customer on the date pro-mised. But it is beginning to break down. It does not allow for the creative movement of ideas, and the growing university population, which includes many girls, is in revolt against the old male-dominated authoritarian paternalism. A high-school headmistress gave me these figures which illustrate the change. Five years ago, for every five girls leaving her school, two went to work, two went home, and one went to university. Now one goes to work, none go home, and four go to university.

But the Japanese are not finding it easy to adopt new and democratic ways. 'We hesitate on the edge of freedom,' a psychologist said to me. 'We do not really know what it is.' He went on to say that 'in Japan the most precious human relations are on the vertical and not on the horizontal plane'—that is to say, the relations between father and son, teacher and pupil, employer and worker, pastor and congregation are more precious and intimate than those between friends of the same age. 'Our myths are generally about obeying and respecting authority, like the myth of the giant snake with nine heads which demanded one person to eat every month. The people of the city had to obey, and they were surrounded by anxiety and fear. Probably the story comes from a river which overflowed and swallowed people. It was no use fighting the river—you could only escape by going away.'

Together with this tradition of obedience there is the formality of Japanese life. The language itself is formal, which makes it difficult for a Japanese to express his feelings except in a formal way. For example, there are many forms for the word 'you', one for inferiors, another for equals, another for superiors, and yet others for the superior of my superior, or for a superior with whom I am in no way connected, such as the emperor. The thinking is hierarchical, so that you cannot talk to the man himself, but only to the man in his social status; and you yourself who address him, you too are not so much an individual as a member of a group—you are a farmer or a worker or a university professor.

Underneath this formality the Japanese are highly

sensitive, and their sensitivity is beautifully expressed through the 'tea ceremony', when every action is formal but the whole ceremony speaks of a deep respect for each other. The guest enters humbly through a low door, so that he is constrained to bow to his hostess. He sits and admires a flower arrangement, while she prepares the tea in a series of ritual and formal movements. When all have drunk, the guest will inquire courteously about her beautiful teapot, and she will tell him where and by whom it was made. The pattern of this ceremony expresses peace and harmony—a quietness in which people may learn to respect each other.

Perhaps the Japanese have in this mutual respect a deep insight into the meaning of participation which they will in time share with the rest of the world. To be part of a crowd queuing for a train in Tokyo during the rush hour is to experience something of this same quietness and respect for each other. Meanwhile, the central problem for the next generation is to translate this participation into social and political terms.

My second hypothesis, about the new shape of the church, was equally confirmed. The existing pattern of church life in Japan is that of the nineteenth century, for although there were Japanese Christians in the sixteenth century, it was only with the modernization of the country a hundred years ago that they were allowed to organize themselves openly. Naturally and inevitably, they built European-looking churches and gathered congregations. A Japanese sociologist told me that up to the last war the church attracted people because it satisfied their social needs. It offered freedom between the sexes, it taught English, and it provided for the enjoyment of music—these were the three introductions which led on to baptism. Today, freedom is established between the sexes, and families have a television set which offers them English and music. 'The ministers must learn the social needs of today,' he said, 'the *real* needs. They are far too theoretical.'

The people of Japan are hungry for religion, as is proved by the new outreaches of Buddhism, which are gaining converts by the million. They seek for the 'recovery of value' (*So-ka-ga-kai*), which includes both perfection of character, or Buddha-hood, by following the teachings of Buddha, and also social service and a concentration on the needs of the poor. A 'temple' built recently in Tokyo expresses architecturally the fact that its congregation is based on the small group. The temple is built like a great circular theatre, of which the auditorium consists of a tier of balconies one above the other, each divided into compartments where a group of up to thirty can meet and talk intimately. The followers of this new 'way' will visit the temple for several hours, and part of this time they will spend in their small groups discussing questions of faith or personal and social problems; they then have only to turn round to become a huge congregation, who can listen to a speaker or worship together.

The Christian church is also adapting and changing into new patterns. Here are three examples.

1. Minoru Ishimaru is a minster in a new area of development, where the population is to grow to three million by 1985. In face of this vast challenge, he started by working in the area for six months as a factory hand and for another six months as a taxi driver. When he had begun to understand the local situation, and a few people had begun to trust him, he founded the Kaiu Culture and Education Centre. Here he provides a kindergarten, and a meeting point for young people and adults —they can meet for dancing, recreation, discussion of social questions and training for social work. In particular

he has set up a Labour Training School, mainly for workers, but also as a point where labour and management can meet each other. The government gives a grant towards his work because it recognizes it as socially useful, but most of the money comes from the participants. In years to come he plans a building many storeys high which will include a church, and later five other such centres in the area, so that there will be two for each city of a million people. This is a striking example of a crumb of yeast leavening the whole lump.

2. On the mountain-side above Kyoto, the ancient capital of Japan, a conference house has just been opened called the Kansai Seminar Centre. Kyoto has a population of about a million, of whom 5,000 are Christians (this is the national average of 0.5 per cent), but the influence of this centre will be out of all proportion to the size of the community which built it. It is beautifully furnished, with a private shower and a telephone in each bedroom, with equipment for instantaneous translation in the conference room, and modern Japanese art on the walls. Here will be another link in the world chain of Christian meeting points, and perhaps the most significant meeting that was being planned at this new centre was one between North and South Koreans. Their countries are divided by a barrier, on either side of which one population is brainwashed against the other. Even when they find themselves living together in Japan, they do not communicate; they set up separate schools for their children who may not even play football against each other. Here in the Kansai Seminar Centre a few of them were at least to meet and talk together, and another tiny crumb of yeast might begin its work of fermentation, with unpredictable consequences.

3. Satoshi Hirata has lived for ten years in a suburb of Osaka, Japan's second largest city. As a graduate he had

started work in a shipyard; from there he went to seminary and was ordained. 'For the next five years,' he said 'I was listening, and making contact, and establishing trust. Then I was invited to help with labour training, because they knew I was skilled in education, and was not trying to get people to church. Industry is changing so rapidly that workers are bewildered and don't understand what is happening. They want training, first, in the implications of their own job—but then we can go further afield, and it becomes a general-culture course. We meet twice a week for eight weeks, and though at first they have the bad Japanese habit of respecting their professor and not thinking themselves, our little group breaks down their isolation, and gives them spontaneity, and we experience fellowship together. The church wants me to come back', he went on, 'and perhaps it is true that in my whole life I shall not make any Christians. But—I am working under the Bible.' Alongside these labour training groups he has also his fellowships for Christian workers, and with them discussion turns into prayer. 'Prayer can be merely a formal beginning and ending to a meeting' he said, 'but we find that having discussed our work we want to pray about it together. At our Sunday meetings one person is assigned each time to talk about his work, and then we are linked together in prayer as we disperse for the next week.'

My last morning in Japan was on Sunday, and I was privileged to be present at such a meeting at Satoshi Hirata's house, in a back street in a poor quarter of the city. There were about sixteen of us, sitting on the floor in a circle, and we included a nurse, two teachers, a shop-assistant, a printer, an electrician and his wife, another housewife, a student of theology, a railway clerk, a business man, two factory workers and a union official. We were about half male and half female, and mostly young. A girl led the service and Satoshi, squatting on the floor like the rest of us, gave a talk which he illustrated on a blackboard by his side. Then we had a time for extemporary prayer; and as we prayed for each others' work and for the needs of the city the barriers between us fell away, and we became for an instant the thing we were praying for—a company through whom the Spirit of Love, like a river, was flowing into Osaka to transform it.

HONOLULU

Twenty-four hours later I was in Honolulu, but as we had crossed the date-line it was still Sunday. So, rather reluctantly, I went to church again. It was a large Gothic building, and the congregation drove up in big cars. Inside, they stood in rows so that they could not see one another's faces, while from far away in front of us prayers were read. After the service we went and drank coffee, and criticized the worship. The contrast with Satoshi Hirata's house-meeting was so sharp that, for a terrible moment, what we were doing seemed a blasphemy.

But it was simply the old, familiar pattern of the church —and once I could attune myself to the fact that I was back in Christendom, I discovered that this particular service was original and exciting. It was Youth Sunday. A special choir of young people was singing modern music composed for the occasion, and two teenagers, a boy and a girl, were speaking to us in place of the sermon. 'We enjoy this affluent world,' they were saying, 'but we didn't create it. It was handed to us. It isn't really ours.' (My ears pricked; where had I heard that before?) 'We need goals to achieve which are our own goals.' Yet at the same time they were pleading for co-operation between the generations. 'We must improve communications,' they said.

I had only been in the U.S.A. an hour, and these were the first Americans I had heard speaking, but already my two hypotheses[1] were being confirmed in yet another country.

LOS ANGELES

In Los Angeles I discovered that these two insights about the city and the church had already been brought together and fused into a common plan of action through the friendship of a city planner and a minister of religion, Calvin Hamilton and John Wagner.

Los Angeles is a great sprawl of a city, ugly and unplanned, with its smog, its traffic congestion and its ghettos. Calvin Hamilton, the Chief Planning Officer, is a man of vitality and vision, and he knows that it is now technically possible to put these things to rights. He also knows that, for the first time in human history, a city need not just evolve blindly, but can decide between various alternative futures, and he believes that the people themselves must participate in this decision. So he has launched the 'Los Angeles Goals Project', by which the inhabitants of the city are asked to share in the formulation of their own future.

John Wagner heads up the 'Inter-Religious Committee' of this Goals Project. The religious bodies have joined together and discovered that, thus united, they are the only organization that can cross all boundaries and penetrate into all levels of city life. At the local level they have set up 'centres for choice' in churches and synagogues, where people can come and discuss the critical issues. But they can also promote dialogue across the city—for example, the ghetto meeting with the business area, to talk about employment and transport to and from work. At the metropolitan level the bishops and other presidents can

[1] See p. 76.

84

bring together those who are involved in city-wide problems, and can invite them to face up to collision courses.
For example, 10,000 people have to leave Los Angeles
every year because of smog, and 70 per cent of smog is
caused by automobiles. Health and the automobile are
on a collision course, and the chief actors in this drama
can be helped to understand the facts, and to discover that
they need each other to avoid disaster.

So here, I discovered, was a city at the heart of which
lay the problem of participation, and here within it was
the church acting in its modern role, offering its specialist
social service, and helping to open up the creative possibilities of participation at the heart of that city. The
planner and the minister were both men of integrity, and
independent of each other. Their enemies were passing
snide remarks, hinting that the planning officer was under
the thumb of the church, or that the church had sold its
soul to the devil of planning. In fact they were friends
—from which very simple fact great benefit ensued to
Los Angeles. They enjoyed eating together, and going on
holiday together with their wives and children. This
made possible a cross-fertilization of their ideas, which
helped the planner to keep in mind the human aspect of
planning, and the minister to understand the social and
political context in which he must work out his gospel of
love.

I saw him doing this one evening. John Wagner took
me to what he called a 'black think tank', which turned
out to be a little group of experts who put their talents at
the disposal of the black community. They asked the
leaders from the ghetto, 'What is your most urgent
problem?' 'Transportation' came the reply, 'the difficulty of getting to and from work.' So for the rest of the
evening we discussed what action they could take. A
sociologist explained how to operate a survey: 250 people

would be needed, who could give ten hours each. He himself would help draw up the questionnaire, and would train them in the use of it. Then, armed with facts, they must approach the city's Transport Committee—and here another member of the 'think tank' offered to draw up a 'sociogram', showing the names of the Transport Committee members, the interests of each, and who spoke to whom. The whole operation was to be organized by the black leaders, and directed by them, and the ultimate purpose went beyond the winning of a better transport service. Two hundred and fifty people in the ghetto would participate, and would gain in confidence and self-respect as they experienced their own power to bring about change through taking political action.

CHICAGO

Some miles north of Chicago, on the shores of the great lake, lies the suburb of Winnetka with its woodlands and its gracious houses. Here I gave my three lectures to the congregation of Christ Church. The audience was composed mainly of intelligent, charming and wealthy people who wielded great power in the city, and who were very humbly asking how they could serve it better. It seemed to me that an enormous potential for good was locked up in that congregation, and I advised them for a start to shut the church building three Sundays out of four, and to meet in small groups where they could open themselves to each other. Out of such meetings might flow a river of understanding love and practical service into the city of Chicago. I don't think they took my advice.

In a run-down area, near the city centre, is a training school where Christian ministers and laymen are learning to plunge right into the poverty of the city. Before he can come on a course, a potential student has to do research into his home situation, analysing the local problems and suggesting possible courses of action. Then, on his arrival at the Urban Training Centre, he takes what is called the urban plunge, which means that with six dollars in his pocket he goes out into the city on Tuesday morning at 10.30 a.m. and he may not come back till 9 p.m. on Friday night. For those four days and three nights he has to live with the poor as one of them. He is shabbily dressed. He grows a beard. He doesn't ask too many questions, he just floats along where the current takes him, earning a bit of money, queuing up for a meal at a Salvation Army hostel, sleeping in an all-night cinema. The theory behind this plunge, as the director of the school told me, is threefold. First, it is shock therapy, forcing middle-class people to see what poverty really is, and what it feels like to be on the receiving end of the church's charity. Secondly, it opens their eyes to see that many of those who are labelled incapable are really quite strong, and during these four days they have the experience of being cared for by people whom they have always thought of as needing care. Thirdly, when they get back, it is pointed out to them that they have only seen what they are capable of seeing.

I talked with a young priest who had taken this plunge. 'It was one of the most rewarding things I have ever done', he told me. He had sat for a while in a labour office, observing who came in and went out. Then he had taken a job, which made him cold, hungry and exasperated with the man in charge, and had helped him to understand why labourers don't come back on the second day. He had refused to enter a Christian rescue centre, because he would have been expected to sing hymns and join in prayers. He had slept one night in a movie-house, and another with a group of hippies, where he had learned to respect their communal way of life. They deliberately deprive themselves of privacy, he said, so that they may be exposed to each other as human beings. They share what little food they have. They make room for a new-comer on the floor, and share their blankets and clothing if it is cold. They abandon themselves to a situation where they have to be forbearing and long-suffering with each other. They crash through the barriers of race, and act naturally and calmly together, and they have no creed, except that nobody is to be excluded. He had asked one girl, who had a job as a waitress, if she was going to live like this all her life. No, she replied, she hoped to marry and live in an apartment and have children—but in a community of others who like herself had learnt to reject false values; because what they had discovered about themselves and other people, and about giving and forgiving, was beautiful—and they must not lose the reality.

At the end of this plunge, the students meet again at the Centre and celebrate the Holy Communion together, breaking the bread and remembering the man who was the friend of outcasts, who 'made himself nothing, assuming the nature of a slave ... and in obedience accepted even death.'[2]

For the next three weeks they work in a small group with a tutor, evaluating their experience, pressing for more information, and finally producing a plan of action for their home situation, which is then criticized by their group and finally by the whole school. The role of the tutor is not to provide the answers. 'We help them', said the director, 'to analyse what are the major problems in the area where they work, and to create *structures* through which people can work out their own answers to their own problems.' After a month at home, testing out his

2 Philippians 2: 7–9 (N.E.B.).

plan, the student may return for a second and even a third term.

At this Urban Training Centre I met a man who had taken a total urban plunge, not just for four days but for his life, and a plunge which involved not only himself but also his wife and family. He did not need 'shock therapy' —that had already been administered by the Gestapo, for he was by race an Austrian Jew named Richard Hauser. He happened to be at the school as a visiting lecturer, and his lecture seemed to sum up all that I had been searching for round the world. He spoke about helping people to think and to do things for themselves—but this was no longer theory, he was telling us *how*. How to prove to people that they are not daft or second-rate. How to take the step out of merely existing ('nothing ever happens in this bloody dump') into living. How to rouse people's curiosity and indignation, and to find leaders, and to form democratic groups, and to do surveys which lead into action so that people may develop solidarity, and courage, and logic and hope.

The leaders of the black community were ready to listen to this white man because he was, in a sense, one of them. He had been knocked about by arrogant thugs who thought themselves racially superior, so now he was able to speak very bluntly to the American Negroes, and to say to them, 'Don't try and show the white men you are as good as they are. Be confident that you are better. Feel gentle towards your victimizers. Teach them, by showing them, that you are morally superior.' I discovered later that Richard Hauser lives on the top floor of a Quaker settlement in the East End of London. Here he and his wife keep open house by day—to help children, advise tenants' groups, train community workers—and are ready to sit up all night with lonely old people who are dying. He is an aggressive and provoking man. He is neither a practising Jew nor a practising Christian in the formal sense, but claims rather forcibly to be an atheist—and rather unconvincingly, because he and his wife (who for full measure is the world famous concert pianist Hephzibah Menuhin) are busy practising love.

WASHINGTON

My last port of call was Washington, and here, at this political nerve centre, I heard a final word about participation and about the role of the church.

It was a few weeks before the assassination of Martin Luther King. Racial tension was increasing, and an American Negro said, 'It's not integration we want, it's participation. The United States is not an enormous melting pot into which you can just drop Indians, Japanese, Chinese, Negroes; we don't come into the pot as equals, but in a master-slave relationship. We want our separate identity—but no hatred. We want to co-operate in creating a new America, and this we can never do if we go the way of violence, because violence may seem to succeed for a moment, but it only creates a reaction of more violence, and then we deteriorate into a police state. We want to go back to the original dream of an America where men are different, but where they have a common goal. We want America to be itself. This is possible on a basis of forgiveness, and the recognition that there is a common need to which all of us can make a contribution.' Then he added emphatically, 'The church must not try to capture this movement.'

This needed saying. If the church is to encourage participation then it really must do this for the sake of other people, and not in an attempt to promote its own life. The aim is not 'capturing' people, but setting them free to be responsible and active, and then leaving them to get on with it. 'It is for your good that I am leaving you',[3] said Jesus—otherwise his mission would have been no more than the old paternalism in a new disguise. Only when he had gone could his spirit take hold of his friends, and lead them into their own discovery of truth. So the final success of the church is its own total disappearance.

But success is too glib a word, and so is disappearance. The ultimate success may only come through disaster, and disappearing may involve being torn in pieces. It was in this city with its acute racial tension that a parish priest spoke the final word about the role of the church. He had an 'integrated' congregation—and for as long as possible, he said, the Christian must go on accepting and understanding both sides. He must hold on to both and refuse to let go till he is literally torn apart. 'Don't talk to me about reconciliation,' he said, 'it's too bland.' In the end reconciliation will not come until somebody has been torn apart and done to death, because not till then will men come to recognize the deep springs of prejudice and self-interest which are in themselves—and in such a moment what they will want to discover will be not reconciliation, but forgiveness.

'Meanwhile,' he said, 'we must celebrate. The structures may collapse but it's only out of chaos that creation comes. We must be happy, and rejoice, and affirm creation and the goodness of man. Every Sunday must be a party. Good *can* come out of evil, and as we break the bread, we are celebrating the hope that is already true.'

So my journey ended. Forty days earlier I had set out round the world to discover the problem at the heart of the city. Now, my mind saturated with information, and suffering from triple culture shock, I discovered that the

[3] John 16: 17 (N.E.B.).

heart of the city is not after all a problem but a celebration —or perhaps, in hippy language, a flower, *'Before milk-white, now purple with love's wound, and maidens call it love-in-idleness'*—a festival of perfect joy—participation in a party.

7. Preparation

THESE CONCLUSIONS about participation and the festival now formed the basis on which we prepared for the conference itself.

THE THEME

While I had been travelling, reports had come in from the workshops, and they represented the jumble which the world is. Some were beautifully produced booklets in glossy folders, while others consisted of a few duplicated sheets of poor-quality paper. Some were erudite and professional, and one at least was written by a trained sociologist. Others were racy, colourful and easily written. Others, again, were heavy and difficult, as though wrung out of the soul of a group who had struggled section by section to discover what it was they wanted to say, and how they could communicate it. Some were written by people who did not know English very well; their language was stilted, but had unexpected turns of speech which shed sudden light. Others were written in foreign languages—the workshop in Brazil, for example, had translated our syllabus of study into Portuguese before tackling it, and had then written a report in Portuguese which had to be translated back into English.

All this raw material was read by a research student, David Boswell, who analysed and summarized it with

93

astonishing accuracy.[1] From this summary it appeared that there were three problems common to every city in the world. The first we called *Social Divisions*—the divisions of race, class, religion, education, age-groups and the like, which appear to be a cause of tension in every city. The second we called *Houses and Homes*—this picked up the basic theme of building decent houses and environment, but included also the question of the family and what is happening to it all over the world under the pressures of city life. The third was *Participation*—the theme which had forced itself upon me during my journey, and which now emerged with equal clarity from the reports.

With some confidence, for we had first-hand and up-to-date evidence, we decided that these were the common problems of the world's cities, and would therefore form the subject matter of the conference.

THE PARTICIPANTS

For a reason which will be explained later, the number of participants was limited to 150. First claim upon these places belonged to the workshops, and we invited two representatives from each city that had sent a report. This would produce about fifty delegates—the other 100 places we allocated to church leaders, secular resource men and students. The church leaders would be on their way to Europe from all over the world, to attend the General Assembly of the World Council of Churches in Sweden, and this looked like being a heaven-sent opportunity to draw together some of the best minds in the church, and give them an occasion to meet some of the secular experts in urban affairs. But when we examined the list of delegates to the General Assembly we were disappointed. It was heavily weighted with

[1] His analysis is reproduced in the Supplement.

'stuffed shirts' and secretaries of this and that, and did not include many of the prophetic people who are actually making experiments on the frontiers of change; however, a careful selection obtained some excellent delegates. For our 'resource men' we approached a number of governments, who sent civil servants, and we issued direct invitations to particular architects and planners, university professors, psychologists, artists, businessmen, economists and others who we believed would have a special contribution to make. The number was made up by students of many different races, most of whom were already studying in Britain. The final list of participants was drawn from thirty-three countries.

We were now faced with the problem of finance. Many of those who wanted to come could not afford to pay the fare, and to achieve the quality of membership at which we aimed it was absolutely necessary to raise some thousands of pounds. This proved difficult, as Britain was going through one of her periodic economic crises. The rich were being severely taxed, and industry found it embarrassing to be asked to pay the fare to Britain of a South American or an Asian at the very moment they were laying off local workers. The public at large was not interested, and the church was too busy financing its existing structures to spare money for research which might suggest that some of them were redundant. So we approached trust funds, only to discover that what we were doing did not fall within their terms of reference, which had been drawn up in a different era. In the end a number of enlightened individuals in Britain and the U.S.A., two trusts, one newspaper and three companies who had subsidiaries in the countries concerned, provided necessary travel grants. It is worth recording the extreme difficulty of raising money, because it points to the need for a tax reform in Britain, making it possible for contributions to be offered more freely to charity, research and the arts. In the U.S.A. and Japan money is more readily available, in the one case through tax concessions, and in the other through semi-official lotteries. Any country which fails to encourage voluntary initiative is in effect sterilizing its own genius.

THE CONFERENCE

In order that participants at the conference should really participate, we proposed to divide them into working groups of ten. These groups would be as mixed as possible, from different races and professions. They would meet for about two and a half hours a day for the first four days, and this would give a chance for everybody to get to know a few others really well, to make his own contribution, and to penetrate the subject in depth. Each group would have a chairman, briefed to encourage shy members and to restrain voluble ones, and a secretary who would sit silent, and observe, and make a report after each session.

These reports, written on half a sheet of paper, would be read each day by one man, Edward Patey the Dean of Liverpool, whose sole job would be the summing up of the discussion. Every evening he would meet with the chairmen and secretaries to feel the pulse of the whole conference, and on the last day he would bring to a plenary session a summary of what the working groups had said.[2] By this means we hoped that the contribution of every single participant could be heard, and that the truth about the world's cities would bubble up out of the meeting of so many minds. Because not more than fifteen reports could be absorbed by one man, and not more than fifteen chairmen and secretaries could easily communicate with each other, we decided that the total member-

[2] This summary is reproduced in the Supplement.

ship of the conference should not exceed 150, which would give fifteen groups of ten. This seemed to be the largest number of people who could genuinely confer together in a week.

There would be three main speakers: Dr Doxiadis to open with a survey of the whole field, Raymond Panikkar to make a theological assessment in the middle, and Professor Colin Buchanan to speak the final word.

The popular image of the planner today is of a ruthless technocrat, unaware of the needs of ordinary people, and Colin Buchanan is the exact opposite—humble, humane and sensitive. I first met him at lunch in the Institute of British Architects, and asked him whether he thought it was nonsense for the church to be calling a conference about the modern city. 'Not at all,' he said. 'Technically, today, we architects can build more or less anything people want. But what do they want? If you can help us all to answer that question it will be very valuable.' We now invited him to do the almost impossible task of summing up our conference, and at the same time making a major pronouncement of his own views on the subject—it was a measure of his greatness that he succeeded in fulfilling this double assignment.

Other members of the conference were invited to speak for twenty minutes, and to bring us information from different parts of the world.

ASIA—Mr Sivaramakrishnan and Reverend Harry Daniel

EUROPE—Mr Richard Hauser

U.S.A.—Mr Calvin Hamilton and Reverend John Wagner

SOUTH AMERICA—Mr Carlos Sabanes

AFRICA—Mr de Graft Johnson.[3]

---

[3] The substance of these talks is given in the Supplement.

THE FESTIVAL

We hoped to do more than talk about the problems of the city. All these remarkable men and women were coming from all over the world—why should not our week together be a celebration, a festival of the arts? Why should we not participate in a party?

The first essential of a good party is to eat and drink together. The conference would open with a dinner given by the Lord Mayor of Coventry in the medieval city hall, at which the Duke of Edinburgh would welcome the guests to England.[4]

Next the arts. The modern city has opened up for the human race new opportunities to enjoy the arts, and it seemed appropriate that a conference on 'People and Cities' should go beyond mere talk *about* the city and actually demonstrate and enjoy what the city makes possible. At the same time the artists would have a lot to teach us about participation.

Sculpture can sum up the meaning of the city, and form a focus amongst the buildings and the networks which people can actually touch. Much modern sculpture is designed to be romped over by children—here is participation *par excellence*. With the help of the Arts Council we gathered together and placed in the ruins of the fourteenth-century cathedral the work of over twenty living sculptors.

Drama criticizes the city, expresses its hopes and fears and draws attention to the dangers threatening it from within. Modern drama is breaking out from behind the footlights and involving the audience directly and immediately in the dramatic action. For our festival we planned three 'dramatic' events which would illustrate this increasing participation. The first was a twenty-

[4] This speech is reproduced in the Supplement.

minute play, created by local young people, on the theme 'People and Cities' and acted in the porch of the cathedral. The second was a performance in the nave of the cathedral by the 'Theatre-go-round', a group of actors from the Royal Shakespeare Company who get out and about, and play in schools and pubs and clubs. The third was a specially commissioned play, produced in our local civic theatre. The playwright was Mr Edward Bond, a young author of integrity whose last two plays had been banned because of their intolerable exposure of the violence and lack of compassion at the heart of our society. Mr Bond hates all bureaucracy, and in particular the church which he sees as a monster imprisoning the spirit of man. We were confident that a play written by him for planners and clergy would not be a string of platitudes, and we asked him to meet the conference members after the performance and discuss his play with them.

Music creates community, and leads us deeply into the experience of participation. Our festival would include concerts by the children of the city, and by the combined choral societies and orchestras of the county, and finally a piano recital by Hephzibah Menuhin woven into an act of worship.

Finally, worship. Worship must be part of the festival; the first four mornings would begin with a Bible passage on the theme of the city, two expounded by a Jew, two by a Christian, and on the fifth day a conference service would unfold in a series of poetry and prose readings how the city is redeemed by love. But should it be only a part—should not the whole festival, the whole conference, be an act of worship? We could not invite our guests to share in the specific act of Christian worship, which is the breaking of bread, because amongst them were Hindus and Moslems, Buddhists and Jainists, Jews, Communists

99

and Humanists. But a we ate and drank together, as we heard the truth spoken to us by artists, as we searched together for peace and justice in the world, would we not in some sense, be celebrating an act of Holy Communion—would we not be recognizing and giving thanks for the love which springs up out of the heart of the city?

8. Happening

THERE IS NO NEED to write at length about the first six days of the conference, since the reader will find the main speeches and papers in Part II of this book, and those who wish to pursue the inquiry will find further material in the Supplement. During those six days, from Tuesday to Sunday, a brilliant galaxy of speakers were laying out the world situation, giving a vision of what was possible and challenging us to action. The festival was a rich feast for body and spirit. The discussion groups met—engaged —reported. And yet, by the end of the sixth evening, something was still lacking.

Everything was too decorous. Perhaps it was overmuch to expect that in a few days people from so many races and professions could break through into real communication. Perhaps the conference itself was too well organized, too 'paternalistic'. There was no clash, no friction, no anger. Richard Hauser's speech on the Thursday had roused a certain amount of enthusiasm, and equally some hostility when he goaded us with his caustic wit and urged us to get beyond verbalizing and into action. The two speakers from South America and Africa, on the Saturday morning, had hurt the whole conference with their descriptions of poverty and injustice, and of the developing peoples caught in an economic prison from which they could not escape. Edward Bond's play, on the Saturday evening, had shocked with its portrayal of the horror that breaks out in a city when there is no compassion. But still no truth had burst out of the conference.

This is not to say that it had been a failure. 'I am profoundly grateful', wrote a delegate afterwards from one of the developing countries, 'for the contact I had with concerned people from all over the world, involved in one way or another with the problems of "People and Cities", and to become aware of the *common problems* and the different shapes—both things were apparent—of urbanization round the world.' 'One of the most important things I learnt', wrote a delegate from Britain, 'was that there are some very able people practising town planning in developing countries.' Several wrote 'the conference has been one of the outstanding experiences of my life'; and there was, of course, the enjoyment of each other which always makes such an occasion worthwhile. 'The people were marvellous' (a girl student from Asia). 'One has made such marvellous friends!' (a bishop from England).

We had gained insight. Insight into the great opportunity of our time, that we are interdependent citizens of one world. Insight into our common problems: that apathy and violence are growing in our cities; that the gap is widening everywhere between the governors and the governed; that all our institutions are creaking under the impact of rapid change, and must be refashioned if they are to set free the potentialities which are in people. This last was increasingly seen to be true of the church. As one minister wrote afterwards from the United States, 'The human problems today present an unprecedented task to the churches. And no churchman at the conference seemed to have specific ideas of what the churches should be doing in response—except an almost total rejection of what is presently being done. There was consensus that no ideas yet advanced are radical enough, but also that the present church structures do not seem capable of implementing on a significant scale even the new styles of ministry which *are* emerging.'

We had also gained vision. Dr Doxiadis had shown us how to look into the future and to hope, to mobilize our skills and to ask, 'Why not?' The Bishop of Middleton had reminded us of the moment when Moses asked God, 'When the people say to me, who has sent you, what shall I say to them?' Most of the translations give God's answer as 'I am' but the Hebrew verb is dynamic, not static, and God's answer is more accurately. 'Tell them *something is happening*!' From Calcutta, Los Angeles and from cities in every continent, we had been told stories of actual experiments now under way—and if other people could do it, then so could we.

As for the church, it might look moribund, but it was founded upon an event which held the key to the life of the city. A great moment of vision came in the conference service. In the last section of the service, entitled 'The City renews its hope', a young actor read to us the story of how Abraham bargained with God, and persuaded him to spare the city if he could find in it ten just men. A second actor read the prophecy of the one and only just man who would stand alone. 'He was despised, and we took no heed of him . . . yet the blows that fell to him have brought us healing.' A third actor read the story of Jesus, of the one just man who fulfilled the prophecy and actually stood alone. They crucified him—but Jesus kept saying 'Father, forgive them; they know not what they are doing.' Then, in a profound silence, Hephzibah Menuhin played a Bach Sarabande, which started in the minor and moved into the major, and turned the crucifixion into the resurrection—and after the silence a voice proclaimed the vision of the City of Peace: 'I, saith the Lord, will be the glory in the midst of her

... and the streets of the city shall be full of boys and girls playing in the streets thereof.'[1] That night, as delegates from all nations drove home in a bus through the streets of Coventry, they were heard to be singing 'Waltzing Matilda'. Something, perhaps, was beginning to happen.

On the Monday morning we met to hear Edward Patey read to the full conference a summary of the conversations we had been having together in the discussion groups. Now, I thought, truth will burst out of our meeting, and we will sound a trumpet blast to the world.

Edward Patey had done his work with scrupulous care, and had recorded the whole range of the discussion in a masterpiece of accurate reporting. When he had finished Professor Dick Chartier from Buenos Aires exploded in indignation. 'I speak out of the third world', he said, 'and I know that this report reproduces only too faithfully what we have said to each other. We have been mild-mannered and polite. We have tried to mend things within the existing structures, and to play the game according to the existing rules. But from the point of view of the third world the whole conference has avoided the visceral guts issue of our time. There is a deep, sharp cleavage, a struggle, a tension, in the world. We have obscured it. One part of the world is set over against the other—this is the class conflict and struggle of our time and we have not yet begun to be aware of it ... We have made only passing references to the great economic realities—half the world is agonizing on the thin edge of resistance to hunger, and man cannot give himself the luxury of talking about the other values if he has got no bread.' It was no use talking about participation, he told us, if we avoided the fundamental issue of political power. Political power lies with economic power. 'We in

[1] Genesis 18; Isaiah 5: 3; Luke 23; Zechariah 2.

South America', he said, 'are victims of the decisions made in the U.S.A. You call the tune. We cannot be political participants, because you have the economic power.' The conference had implicitly endorsed the *status quo*, and avoided the real issue which was, for the third world, the radical transformation of society. We had been, sociologically, like babes in the wood. 'Is this the level at which an international conference should function, that some member has to turn to another and say "Don't forget to love your neighbour"?'

'Yes,' shouted Dick Hare, Professor of Moral Philosophy at Oxford.

'But what is this love?' rejoined Chartier. 'In our urban world, our secular world, love must be translated into the structures of justice—and this is the joint task of theology and the social sciences.'

Suddenly the conference had opened up, and two of our leading thinkers had expressed their deepest convictions. Professor Hare wrote later, 'I should like to add a final paragraph to my paper, saying that the language which really has to be learnt is the language of morals, i.e. of love [see page 163]. My vociferous "yes" in the middle of Chartier's diatribe will have made the point ... it would be a rare and satisfying achievement to have said all I really wanted to say at the conference in one word.'

Meanwhile other delegates rose in support of Chartier to say, from South Africa, that violence is not just something which breaks out within the system, the whole system itself is violent; to say, from Czechoslovakia (this was a few weeks before the Russian invasion), that the main issue was one of power, and whether or not people could in any real sense participate in the political events of our day. An American Negro pointed out that we had no 'poor people' at our conference. We had talked about encouraging them to participate, but their voice had not in fact been heard. An African told us that unless we paid a fair and stable price to the man in his country who grows a pineapple, it was no good talking to him about participation; it was no good even telling him *how* to participate; he simply would not *be able* to participate, because without the economic resources there would be nothing to participate in.

In face of these sharp and urgent cries, all our discussion began to look rather tame. To issue some general statement or exhortation to the world would be futile. We must *do* something. But what? Another voice from Africa warned us that we didn't yet know what to do (and by this time it was becoming clear that the best contributions were coming from the developing countries). 'We are still like the doctor,' he said, 'who is asking questions. What the patient thinks he wants is something active, some injection or pill to be given immediately. But the doctor knows he must ask questions first and, if he is not sure, he must go on asking questions.'

At this point one of our British members tried in good British parliamentary fashion to move a resolution. It was a fine speech urging us not to resolve that somebody else should do something, but that we ourselves, with all the insight and the vision of this meeting together, should now go forward to action in our local situations. So that we might support each other, and defend those who might be in danger from oppressive régimes, we should keep ourselves in being as a body; and to this end he proposed that for a limited period we set up a secretariat which could act as a clearing house for an international network.

'This is the moment I have been dreading,' said a delegate from Israel. 'The conference resolution! Yesterday I talked for three hours with a boy from Egypt and I didn't need a secretariat to do that. We have had here an experience of freedom, of meeting one another and talking on a person to person basis; let's go back and carry on doing that, and not set up another organization.'

And then, after a few more speeches, the simple statement from Africa which was the turning point. 'I oppose this resolution. I think I don't want any resolutions. I come from the third world but this is not a conference about the third world. It is an international conference and it is about a problem we all have in common. How many times have we blasted the West with speeches about our poverty? But they too are suffering. Their society is decaying. They too need an injection to revitalize them. I believe that the only resolution worth having is the resolution to personal involvement—the resolution to commit ourselves.'

We agreed, overwhelmingly.

This, it seemed, was the conclusion of three years' work and of a world-wide inquiry, that we should publish no statements, and that we should pass no resolutions—not even the resolution to keep ourselves in being. It seemed a bitter moment of failure—we would scatter, and there would be nothing left to show for it. Yet at the very same instant it was a breakthrough into a success far beyond our imaginings. Hampered by no resolutions of the conference, each member was now completely free to react according to his own situation, his own personality, his own understanding of what the week had given him. From that instant one after another rose to his feet to say what he was going to do. We would scatter on the next day, and there would be nothing left to show for it in Coventry, but a fire had been kindled, and we would scatter like sparks to set places alight. We would scatter, not just emotionally committed to an ideal, but with a new knowledge of techniques.

During the hours that followed, I began to appreciate

what power had been let loose. The delegates from Asia held a special meeting, and each one was asked to say what he was going to do. An Indian said, 'I am going back to my city, where we have no planning. We are only a number of overgrown villages. I am going to get together sociologists and psychologists with the City Fathers, members of the Rotary Club, representatives of the trade unions and of managements and other areas of city life to discuss what kind of a city they would like to live in tomorrow. I look forward to an exciting time, not merely to sharing ideas, but to projecting these ideas into a plan, which may in a humble way begin the transformation of our city.' From across the room an Australian architect answered him, 'I have learnt from this conference that the resources of Australia must be at the disposal of Asia. I and my colleagues will come and help you.'

So it has continued. Not alone now, but knit together by a 'happening' into an informal network across the world, the participants are carrying into action and passing on to others what they have learnt.

As I write, a letter from Brazil has just arrived, which makes a fitting conclusion to this chapter.

Our previous workshop has died, only to give birth to a more ambitious project in *action* . . . Before we met at Coventry, we intended to have a sociological survey, to detect the relations (if any) between São Paulo's urban needs, and the resources of the churches which operate in this city. After Coventry, we decided that we should give up our theoretical approach and change the project, transforming it into an experiment in action, in an area hardly touched by the churches here: industrial ministry. We have formed a group of three young ministers (a Presbyterian, a Methodist and myself Anglican) who are prepared to move to an under-privileged neighbourhood to live and work amongst industrial workers. We shall be backed by some of the people involved in the previous workshop, besides quite a few others who are now helping as technical advisers. My wife and I will be moving this month ... we shall conduct an exploratory survey.

I count on your prayers to support us, and shall be glad to receive information on what is going on amongst other 'urban-minded' people around the world.

9. The Shape of the Church in the Modern City

THE STORY is finished, but before handing the reader over to a philosopher, two planners, a social worker and a theologian, I would like to make my own professional contribution as a priest to this discussion of 'People and Cities'.

I hesitate to do this for two reasons. First, because the church has no 'answer' to the problems of the city apart from all the secular professions. I can only hope that this conviction has emerged with utter clarity out of the preceding pages. The reader will understand that by saying 'we are the city' I am not contradicting Professor Buchanan when he says that the city is primarily buildings. It is necessary that a priest should say the one and that an architect should say the other, and that they should be in a personal relationship with each other as they say it—because only in a personal relationship can these insights become one dynamic which is capable of creating the city.

But there is a deeper reason for hesitation. In a sense my professional contribution as a priest is to tell a story, and this follows from the fact that the name of God is *'something is happening'*. To declare that 'something', one must tell a story, one must show the thing actually happening, and the moment one stops telling a story and comments upon it the happening turns into a system and dies. This is the danger when St Paul interprets Jesus, or the church institutionalizes him. But it is a danger which has to be run, and it is not harmful as long as the interpretation is recognized to be less than the story—it is only one meaning, which has struck one mind, and is put into words so that it may be passed on to strike another mind —and as long as the institution continues to be only the means through which the happening continues to happen. So if now I try to describe the shape of the church and its role in a modern city, this must not be taken as a blueprint. It is merely an attempt to interpret, for a moment, some of the meaning of what is happening all over the world today, and to give it expression so that others may grasp hold of it. Perhaps one should say, more accurately, so that others may be grasped by it, and once the idea has taken hold, the blueprint must be torn up, because it will not fit any actual situation.

THE SHAPE OF THE CHURCH

Human nature does not change, but environment does. In all that follows I am not suggesting that the personal message which the church carries to an individual has changed in the last 1,900 years. It is still the good news about Love; that Love cares, Love accepts you as you are, Love sets you free to live. But the environment has become so different in the last 100 years that the structures of the church no longer fit the way people live, and they no longer convey the message.

Throughout its history the church has adapted its outward shape to the changing pattern of society, to be with people and serve them where they are.

In the fourth century, when towns were islands of culture in a sea of paganism, a large church would be built in a town and served by a team, and from this centre itinerant clergy and lay specialists would radiate out into the surrounding countryside. These lay specialists would include doctors, teachers, builders, farmers and the whole team together would meet the total needs, physical and spiritual, of the people to whom they came.

From the eighth to the tenth century, as Europe became more settled, village life developed, and the parish system grew up as we now know it. This system, as we have already seen, was beautifully adapted to settled life in small communities. The parson could know and care for each of his parishioners, and the church stood as the visible centre of the community. During the middle ages, this parish system was supplemented by the monasteries, which provided for the wider needs of the community as centres of learning and services.

Today, the social reality is the city region. What pattern must the church adopt if it is to penetrate into all the complexity of the modern city and be with people and serve them where they are? Here we can be helped by Dr Doxiadis, and the 'ekistic grid' which he has developed, showing that urban society today consists of fifteen different sizes of community, from the home to 'ecumenopolis'. The church in the modern city must be present at all those fifteen levels. But this is only a beginning, for this initial complexity of the city is crisscrossed by other communities which are not geographical, but are based on interests of various kinds. These include the institutions of the city, such as industry and education, which operate over the city as a whole. They include also communities of common interest, such as political parties or the world of sport and the arts, and communities of need such as the old, the lonely, the drug addicts. Finally, there are the immigrant communities that exist in every city today.

But before we begin to suggest a shape for the church which would fit this complexity, we must remember another factor which complicates a modern city even further. This is the fact that its physical lay-out and the composition of its population are in process of rapid change. Motorways may be driven through a city which within a year or two will change its whole pattern of community. And we cannot even predict that development plans will be carried through. An economic freeze, unforeseen changes in industry or population growth, or in the social aims of the political party in power, may cause the plan to be radically changed. Any shape for the church which we propose must itself be flexible, so that it can change with the shape of the city which it serves. The element of stability will have to be provided by the unchanging message of love which the church speaks to an unchanging human nature, and not by the buildings and organizations which it erects in a rapidly changing environment.

Now we will begin to sketch such a shape, taking a few points on the ekistic grid as our starting points.

I. THE STREET

How is the church to be present at this basic level of community? The answer is obvious. The church is present through an individual Christian who lives there. We will suppose, for the sake of the illustration, that this is the only Christian in the street, and at this point let it be said once and for all that, when I say 'the church is present', by the church I mean the whole united body of Christian churches. I have no right to speak for other religions, though the day cannot be far off when we unite for service to the community. But already the time is long overdue when, in face of the urban crisis, all Christians recognize their unity and act upon it, and here at the basic level of community in the street, it is irrelevant whether the Christian is Roman Catholic, Orthodox or Protestant. Will there be any outward manifestation of the church at this level—any church building? Perhaps, in the home of this Christian, a crucifix, an icon, a bible. Worship will take the form of private prayer.

2. THE SMALL NEIGHBOURHOOD

This consists of about 2,000 people, perhaps centred on a primary school. The church is present in the form of a small group, or groups, of Christians. Each group will need a leader, who will be a lay man or woman, and may be leader for one evening, for a year, or permanently—there are no rules about this. One of these leaders may be designated the lay pastor for the neighbourhood. The church building will be an ordinary living-room in some-body's house, used for a meeting. The worship will take the form of bible study, or discussion, or extempore prayer, or silence, or of any combination of these. The groups might decide to meet together occasionally in the local school.

3. THE LARGE NEIGHBOURHOOD

This consists of about 10,000 people, who may be served by one shopping centre. The church will be present in a honeycomb of small cells, each with their lay leader, but at this point on the scale there may be also an ordained minister. He will meet with his 'inner staff' of lay pastors, and will visit house groups. The church building may be his own house, which has attached to it a large meeting room to hold 100. Here will be held meetings for informal worship. Larger meetings can be held in the secondary school, or the community hall.

4. THE TOWN, OR URBAN AREA

This consists of about 50,000 people, and here for the first time we find a church building, where formal worship

is held. It is staffed by a team of ordained ministers, each
of whom has a neighbourhood for which he is pastorally
responsible, and each of whom may have specialist duties,
such as hospital work, or youth work. At about this point
on the scale it begins to be necessary to specialize, since
it is at this level in the city that the social services should
begin to have their local centres.[1]

5. THE CITY

Let us suppose that this consists of half a million
people, or ten urban areas. In addition to the ten local
churches in these areas there will be a centre of celebration
or a 'cathedral' at the city centre, where formal and informal worship will take place, great speakers will be
heard and there will be occasions of music, drama, dancing. This celebration centre will be the base for a team
ministry, each member of which has a specialist role.
Perhaps here I can leave Utopia, and quote the actual
example of Coventry Cathedral, where there is a staff of
clergy and laity (male and female) and each member of
the staff has his specialist function: e.g. industry, commerce, education, drama, youth, immigrants, international affairs, urban mission, worship. Every Monday
morning the staff meets for Holy Communion, breakfast,
Bible study and chores, and as a a result, though each is a
specialist, they are held together in a personal relationship, and within this relationship they hold together the
city. This simple pattern is of profound significance for
the life of a modern city, and is the secret of how the
church may penetrate and serve its complexity.

We could continue with this sketch, ascending through
the city region which is the modern diocese, to the state
or region with its archbishop, to the nation, and to the

[1] See the Seebohm Report 1968.

world with its popes, patriarchs and presidents. Each of these levels is a different kind of community, and has different problems; and the church must be present at each level in an appropriate form—at national level, perhaps, in the form of academies for dialogue, training schools, monasteries, administrative centres; at world level in the form of research centres into the great international problems of the day: hunger, development, trade, war, world government, the population explosion.

We might even dare to draw a diagram, to set beside Dr Doxiadis' diagrams of the city, on condition that no reader take it literally.

Three points should be noted:
a. Everyone in a smaller unit belongs also to a larger unit. For example, the individual in the street also belongs to a neighbourhood, the city, the world.
b. The popes, patriarchs and presidents are put at the bottom and not at the top, to emphasize the type of leadership required of them.
c. The forms of worship are drawn in a different dimension, and do not belong exclusively to any unit of size. For example, silence may be very potent in a cathedral. But it is interesting to note that different forms of worship become possible at different levels.

This diagram suggests the necessary complexity of the church if it is to match the complexity of the urban world. At present Christians tend to think of the church in terms of one unit only from each column, i.e. the congregation, the minister, the church building, formal worship. The complexity of the urban church should not be regarded as a problem, but as an opportunity to break out of one limited experience of fellowship and worship into a far wider range of experiences. People would discover a new health and wholeness of spirit if they could involve them-

	People	Leaders	Buildings	
Street	Person	Person	Crucifix Icon Bible	Private prayer Bible study
Small Neighbourhood	Groups	Lay pastors	Living-room	Extemporary prayer Silence
Large Neighbourhood	Groups Congregations	Ministers	Meeting hall	Informal worship Formal worship
Urban Area	Congregation	Team leaders	Church	
City	City communities	Urban deans	Celebration centre Cathedral	Festive occasions
City Region	Diocese circuit	Bishops Chairmen	Administration Centre	Television Broadcasts
Nation	National church	Cardinals Archbishops Moderators	Academies Training schools Monasteries	Pilgrimages
World	One Holy Catholic Apostolic Church	Popes Patriarchs Presidents	Research centres	Forms of Worship

selves sometimes in a group, at other times in a congregation—if they could learn to worship sometimes alone, at other times together, with extemporary prayer, or in an act of formal worship, or through a pilgrimage.

THE CHRISTIAN COMPANY

The basic shape of the church is the small group. This is not merely true at the neighbourhood level. At whatever level a person may be operating, whatever his temperament, whatever his position in the hierarchy, he needs to belong to a small company to which at least occasionally he can return.

The reason for this is not difficult to see. The very foundation of the human spirit—of being a human person—is our capacity to meet other persons. It is in the moment when I am confronted by another person, and recognize that he is of supreme value, that I become myself. Now this creative meeting of person with person takes place most naturally in a small group, numbering from two to twelve. There is nothing mysterious about this; we all know it to be true. It is recognized in industry, where a managing director will not usually try to be in creative contact with more than six people. It is increasingly being understood in the sphere of healing, where the doctors are discovering the therapeutic power of the small group. Most people experience it directly in a family, or through playing games in a team, and it is interesting to note that in the realm of sport this maximum number of twelve is confirmed; a football or cricket team numbering eleven acts and plays together as a single unit, while a rugger team numbering fifteen is divided into two parts, the scrum and the outsides, each with a healthy contempt for the other.

For the Christian this simple, natural truth is of basic importance, because he believes that the natural can be penetrated and transformed by the super-natural. I use the word 'super' as my children use it, when for example they say we have had a super holiday. This means that the holiday has not just been a series of free days, in which we happened to sit by the seaside. It has had about it some extra sparkle, some quality of joy, of deep peace, of self-enhancement and of love for each other (which includes a certain amount of quarrelling). It has been supremely a holiday. Now Christians believe—and this is the exciting heart of their faith—that the super-natural Spirit of Love can penetrate and transform the spirit of man, making us supremely ourselves.

This belief is based on the event of Jesus, the most super-natural man. The divine Spirit of Love flowed through him like a river, and St Paul, trying to interpret the happening, said 'God was in Christ'.[2]

Now if this is the mode of the Spirit's operation, that the Spirit of Love penetrates and transforms the spirit of man, and if it is also true that the foundation of the spirit of man lies in the deep meeting of person with person, then it follows with inescapable logic that it is through this meeting of person with person that the divine Spirit of Love enters the human situation. The primary responsibility of the church, therefore, in deciding on its shape, is to provide meeting points where this can happen.

When a small company of people begin to meet and act around Jesus rather than, let us say, around a football, then they too experience what has been called the 'harvest of the Spirit'.[3] The first fruit of the Spirit is *love*. As they have the courage to open themselves to each other, they move from prejudice and jealousy towards an understanding and respect for each other, and into a need for one another as partners in a great task. The

[2] Corinthians 5: 19 (N.E.B.).
[3] Galatians 5: 22 (N.E.B.).

second fruit is *truth*. As they share what little knowledge each one has, they are grasped together by a single truth which no one of them could have known by himself. The third fruit is *joy*. As they accept each other, each one begins to accept himself—he becomes less pompous, less afraid. The fourth fruit is *peace*, and this is the heart of the matter, for as they meet more intimately together, so they are driven up harder against one another, and they experience that tension which is at the heart of human affairs. They realize their own selfishness and aggression. They recognize that 'one is one and all alone, and evermore shall be so'. It is at this point that they will either break up, or experience the terrifying reality of forgiveness, when the football, so to speak, starts kicking the team rather than the team the football, when Jesus stands among them as he promised ('where two or three have met together in my name, I am there among them')[4] and says to them, 'I have chosen you all. I have accepted you. I am sending you out together. Now go and share this forgiveness with other people.'

Until Christians have experienced forgiveness they have no good news for the city. This *is* their good news—their gospel. Tragically, just at the moment when it is most needed, the church is organized in such a way as to make the experience very difficult to come by. Ministers operate singly, instead of in teams, and they invite people to meet in large congregations where they are content to be on nodding acquaintance. The larger the congregation, it is generally considered, the greater the success. But the pressures of the modern city are driving the church back towards its own original prototype. For when its founder created the prototype of the church, he chose a small company of twelve, men of clashing and contrasting personalities, who round him should discover the reality of

4 Matthew 18: 20 (N.E.B.).

forgiveness, and should then go and spread this good news to the ends of the earth.

We must examine, in a concluding chapter, how this role of 'forgiveness' will be acted out in a modern city. But here there are two final points to be made about the shape of the church.

First, that this structure of cells provides the maximum flexibility and diversification, while at the same time preserving coherence. The analogy of the human body suggests an organism made up of millions of cells which are of different shapes and perform different functions, each one a centre of life, yet no one independent of the others. They are all held together in the life of the total body which they together create and preserve. So these cells will be of an infinite variety. If no two snowflakes are alike, and no two people have the same fingerprints, then *a fortiori* no one group of human beings will be exactly like any other group. Some groups may be for study, some for action. They may be prayer groups, house churches, week-end conferences, holidays together, pilgrimages, lunch clubs, supper clubs—some meeting weekly, some monthly, some three times a year, some once only and never again—in any of an enormous variety of ways and constantly shifting patterns by which person can meet person and be together at the disposal of the Spirit of Love. This is not the only shape of the church—each person also has an absolute need for privacy, and for formal worship, and for authority. But here, in the cell, is the basic meeting point where he can be penetrated and transformed by the Spirit of Love.

The second point is this. The best name for these groups is probably not 'cell' but 'company'. A cell is the place where life takes its first positive form; the word can also have a rather subversive sense, as of a cell of revolutionaries, and many Christians today believe that this must now be their role. But in the end we are not a resistance movement, we are persons sitting down to give thanks for a victory, to celebrate the sure and certain hope that 'something is happening', to break bread together. A company is, literally, a body of people who break bread together[5]—and this action most perfectly expresses our shape and, as we must now see, declares our role.

[5] Latin, *com* (together) + *panis* (bread).

10. The Role of the Church in the Modern City

'SOMETHING is happening', but it is dangerous to define it. If I now make three propositions, these are not supposed to provide a total definition of the role of the church in the modern city, so that we can then sit back and say 'Ah! Now we know. The work is finished.' They are rather some signposts towards action, or springboards from which to take an urban plunge.

I. THE GENIUS OF THE CITY IS COMPLEXITY

One of the most important things we have now to do is to reinstate the word complexity as a 'good' word. As we have already seen, it originally means 'to embrace', and the complexity of the city lies not only in its buildings and its networks, but also in the opportunity for lots of people to embrace each other in a variety of human relationships. The truly urban man, as somebody said to me in Los Angeles, is the man who welcomes complexity, and responds to it with his whole personality.[1]

The complexity of the city demands two things: both that each individual develops his full potentialities, and

---

[1] Cf. *Community Work and Social Change*, report by the Calouste Gulben-kian Foundation, Longmans 1968, p. 79: 'Variety in a society is a good to be welcomed in its own right'; and p. 85: 'Belief in the value of diversity in human life lies at the base of the idea of self-determination in social work.'

also that all the citizens care for one another and serve each other responsibly. These are the two goals of the city on which everybody is agreed—whether you ask a Christian, a Communist or a Humanist, he will give you these same two answers. But they are not only the goals, they are also the processes leading towards the goal and going on all the time.

The city does, in fact, provide for the individual citizen a wide variety of opportunities through which he can develop his particular talents: colleges which offer him specialist training in everything from business studies to music; schools for the blind, the deaf, the mentally handicapped; an almost infinite variety of work, housing, services, recreation, friends. Many barriers, by which in former generations he was hemmed in, have now fallen away. Through jet travel he can overcome the outward barriers of space, and through television, even if he cannot travel, he can press a button and see into other continents or be introduced to new people and new ideas. Through psychology he can at least understand the inward barriers which have divided us from each other for so long, the barriers of suspicion, prejudice and fear.

The individual has the opportunity as never before to develop his potentialities; but equally the city community as a whole is seen to be a continuous marvel of co-operation. Apart from occasional lapses, the electricity works, the buses run to time, the shops have the goods we need, children are taught, music is played, and a host of decent neighbours turn and help one another in time of need.

The genius of the city is complexity—or to use another word, which is also misused and devalued, the genius of the city is love. This love, this embracing, is more than sex. 'Love is the willing communication to others of that which we have and are,' wrote Brooke Foss Westcott.[2] 'Love is the accurate estimate and supply of somebody else's need,' wrote C. F. Andrews. These two definitions of love describe the true complexity of the city in personal and social relations.

The first is the secret of a full individual personality, for as we have seen, it is in 'meeting' others that a man becomes himself, and this meeting is in the end the 'willing communication to others of that which we have and are'. But further, if communication, as Professor Hare thinks, is the *raison d'être* of the city, then behind all the technical questions involving traffic, telephones, mass media, there lies at the heart of the city the problem of love. Behind the question, 'How can we communicate?' lie the further questions, 'Do we want to communicate?' and, 'What have we to communicate?' In the last resort, as public relations men know, you do not communicate through circulars or party manifestos, but through one person who meets another and wills to communicate himself.

But if we confined ourselves to this first definition of love, our city would be lop-sided. The second—'the accurate estimate and supply of somebody else's need'—is the secret of a responsible society. Simon Phipps, commenting on this definition, writes: 'It drains the word [love] of emotion and of inadequately grounded optimism. It implies accurate analysis and diagnosis, leading to effective remedy ... This accurate, professional, unsentimental, realistic assessment of situations leads to the sort of good results which are worth calling "love".'[3] This kind of love in action which is the secret of a responsible society, is also the fulfilment of the individual 'urban' man, who moves beyond meeting and into

---

[2] *The Epistles of St John.* Additional note on I John 3: 16.
[3] Simon Phipps, *God on Monday*; Hodder and Stoughton 1966.

action as he 'responds to complexity with his whole personality'.

These two, communication and responsible service, are the twin aspects of *participation,* the word which we have used up to this point to express the problem at the heart of every modern city in the world today. But participation is an ugly long jargon word. From now on we will use shorter and more attractive words, and say that at the heart of the city is the problem of complexity or love.

For a problem, unfortunately, there is. It would be equally dangerous to look at the city through rose-coloured spectacles or through dark glasses. But if we look at it realistically with the naked eye, we can see that its great promise is only partially fulfilled. It misses the mark. Individual people in the city too often do not realize their full potentialities, but are lonely and afraid, stereotyped, hopeless, dwarfed by the size of it all. They take drugs and fill the mental hospitals. They are twilight people, not fully alive. And the responsible society is too often marred by irresponsibility. People shut themselves off from each other. They retire behind their racial and class prejudices. They pollute the atmosphere with smoke and petrol fumes. They choke up the streets with private cars. They slash trees, sell each other shoddy goods, divorce their husbands or wives, and leave things to the government—which gets more and more remote, and bribes people at election time with promises which it does not fulfil. There is, in short, a failure within society to fulfil obligations and to keep faith with each other.

Now there is an old word which exactly expresses this twofold failure—both the failure of the individual to become what he has it in him to be, and also the failure within society to keep faith with each other. It is the word *sin*. If one has hesitated to use the word 'complexity' and the word 'love', how much more does one hesitate to use this word 'sin', for it has been perverted from its original sense, and in its false meaning quite rightly rejected by this generation. However, instead of inventing another word, we would do better to reinstate it in its proper meaning. The accurate definition of this ancient Judaeo-Christian concept is:

a. The failure to be yourself. To sin is to miss the mark, to be off target.
b. The failure to keep faith with others. To sin is to break an agreement or contract. It is to injure the community.

The word 'sin' expresses, with astonishing accuracy, what is wrong with the modern city. By saying this we are not necessarily blaming anybody in particular. A man may be driven into a mental hospital because he has been declared redundant by his company in an economic crisis. A boy may slash a tree because he has no proper outlet for his natural aggression. By saying that all this is sin, we are merely stating that here, in the city, whether or not people are individually responsible, is a failure to achieve the city's twofold goal.

But an accurate definition of the word 'sin', as used in the early Jewish and Christian writings, includes a third element. Sin is rebellion against God. Here we are up against the most difficult of all words. If we are to understand what the Jews and the Christians originally meant by the word 'God', we might say with the Jews that the name of God is 'something happening', and with the Christians 'God so loved that he gave'. Sin would then be rebellion against what is happening, or rebellion against Love that gives. In city terms, it would be to set up oneself, or any form of society, against the irresistible

power of self-giving love which is in the city and expressing itself through the city.

If the ailment is sin, then the cure is forgiveness. This
brings us to the second proposition, in which we discover
the role of the church.

2. WHAT MAKES COMPLEXITY WORK IS FORGIVENESS

Here again is a word that has been emasculated. Forgiveness does not mean that some morally superior person
stoops down to one who is in the wrong, and says,
'Never mind. I will forget it.' Once we have discovered
the true meaning of sin, we can understand immediately.
that such a condescending attitude would not help at
all. If sin is my failure to become myself, then what I
need is encouragement to become myself. If sin is a broken
contract with my neighbours, then what we both need
is that personal relations between us should be restored.
If sin is setting up myself or my society against Love, then
what we all need is that Love should once again be in
control, expressing itself through our complexity, flowing through ourselves and our city like a river.

In expressing these three needs we have given an
accurate description of forgiveness as we can see it
'happening' in the life of Jesus. This is precisely what he
did. He encouraged frightened people to be whole. He
brought divided people back into unity. He opened up
the river of Love to flow through them. 'Whoever believes
in me,' he said, 'streams of living water shall flow out
from within him.'[4] He was speaking of the Spirit of Love
which would be liberated by his death.

To continue this work of forgiveness is precisely the
role of the church in the modern city, and it answers
exactly to the city's deepest need. In concrete terms, this

[4] John 7: 38 (N.E.B.).

involves helping people to meet each other, at all the levels of community which we showed in the diagram. In the street, a new neighbour moves in; within a short time, unobtrusively, somebody has welcomed him; he feels he belongs and that he is needed. In the city centre, a group of industrial managers, foremen, trade union officials and shop stewards meets to talk out their basic attitudes to automation; they are on neutral ground; they need not make speeches at each other; they can joke together, and get to know each other as real people. So the ferment activates, all over the city, helping people to understand each other and to grow in tolerance; and as they find themselves accepted by each other, so they are no longer afraid, they become less rigid, and are able to accept themselves and to co-operate freely together in the service of the city. Complexity works. The infinitely creative power that lies within people and cities is unlocked.

But forgiveness is not simply a matter of meeting and talking together. As we have already seen in the 'shape of the church', the reality of forgiveness is only to be known through tension and an agonizing self-awareness, and if the 'role of the church' is to share this experience with others, then it can only be by standing with them at that same point of agony. To encourage people in the city to meet each other is in the end to go with them to the place where their deep instinct of aggression is laid bare, their financial interests are threatened, their inherited prejudices are challenged. At such a point of tension forgiveness involves holding on to both sides even if it means being torn in pieces—and that may sometimes be necessary in order that men may come to complete self-awareness and to a full recognition and acceptance of Love.

This change-over to self-awareness, this coming on-target, is called in technical theological language 'repentance'—another word which needs reinterpreting, for it means not so much becoming aware how bad I am or how bad the city is, as recognizing how good both I and the city have it in us to be. Repentance is the recognition of Love, and that the heart of all our complexity (or embracing) is *Love embracing us*; and it issues in the putting of ourselves at Love's disposal, and the realization in common action that together we can be the channel through which the river of Love flows into the city. We are the river. We are the city. This may sound mystical, but it is in fact coming near to the language of the biologist. Evolution, biologists tell us, seems to them to be like a river flowing through all life in a certain direction. What we are suggesting is that both the river and the direction, both the process and the goal, are Love; and the role of the church is to co-operate in the processes and to be a catalyst breaking down old patterns and creating new, and itself being broken up and recreated in the process. As we commit ourselves to this process and this goal in action, so forgiveness is already completed, because the rebellion is over, and Love is once more in control, expressing itself through our complexity.

'Meanwhile,' as my friend in Washington had said, 'we must celebrate the hope.' We must throw a party in honour of Love. To worship is to recognize what is 'happening', to give thanks, and to put ourselves together at Love's disposal. Such worship can go on all the time, everywhere, but for Christians it is expressed most perfectly in the breaking and giving of bread.

Which brings us to the third proposition.

3. CHRISTIANS OUGHT TO BE EXPERTS IN FORGIVENESS

I have to write 'ought to be' because often they are not. An 'expert' is literally one who has 'experienced' something, and we need to return to a structure of the church where forgiveness can become our common experience and is the continuing context in which we live. Such a structure, as it is in fact emerging, has been outlined in this book.

Christians ought, nevertheless, to be experts in forgiveness, because their faith is not based on a theory. It is based on a man who actually *did* it. And because he did, they can.

As I went round the world I was asking myself two questions about the city and the church. But privately I was asking myself a third question about my own faith. 'Can I go on saying "Thou who takest away the sin of the world"? Is it true?' I decided that it was. In cities all over the world I saw that 'something is happening'. I found little companies of people who were committed to the work of forgiveness, who broke bread together and said, 'You did it. So I can. And as your representative, I will.'

PART II

Five Wise Men

There was found in [the city] a poor wise man, and he by his wisdom delivered the city; . . . The words of the wise heard in quiet are better than the shouting of a ruler among fools.

ECCLESIASTES 9: 15, 17

(from a Bible passage chosen by Rabbi Schacter and expounded at the 'People and Cities' conference)

Introduction

THE FOLLOWING five chapters comprise edited versions of the two full-length papers given by Richard Hare and Richard Hauser and the three main speeches by Constantine Doxiadis, Colin Buchanan and Raymond Panikkar, given at the 'People and Cities' conference.

These five men were invited to lead the conference because we considered them to be, each in his own field, outstanding interpreters of the modern city. They describe different aspects of the city from different professional standpoints, and yet their descriptions all emphasize a single quality, and focus upon the same characteristic.

Richard Hare describes the city as 'an organism for communication'. The city is something all the people have in common—it is *their* city. They have to hear and understand one another, and learn to speak together the language of peace, morality and love. Constantine Doxiadis sets out the interlocking elements of the city. 'Who is going to build the proper city?' he asks. 'All of us. The city does not belong to any special group of experts. We must mobilize all our resources, and all age-groups, from the artists to the political leaders, including the rebellious students.' Richard Hauser writes of the missing factor of 'human warmth'; of community, tolerance and solidarity; of 'common' sense, and of partners and colleagues in urban living. Colin Buchanan defines an urban area as 'an assemblage of linked buildings occupied by people engaged in a great variety of interdependent activities'. He warns us that 'the function-ing of urban areas is infinitely more complicated than most people have been willing to admit'. The problems are 'highly complicated, interlinked questions, deserving of the scientific approach—deeply involved at every turn with human beings of every description'. Finally Ray-mond Panikkar sees the health of the city as consisting in a 'pluralism which does not disrupt harmony and unity'. He sees man as 'a centre of relationships', who needs in his city 'communion, the awareness of a basic unity', which in turn will lead to the growth of diversity. 'Wisdom', he writes, 'is to detect the true rhythm of things, and joy is to move—to dance—according to that rhythm.'

All these men are describing, in different words, what in the first part of the book I have called the 'complexity' of the city.

Complexity is a term which the planner and the theologian have in common with the biologist, for the biologist sees in ordered complexity the principle of the evolution of life itself. Through his microscope the single cell appears as an almost incredible marvel of complexity. As cells differentiate and specialize, greater complexity makes possible higher forms of life, till the co-operation of some thousands of millions of cells in man's brain pro-duces our human consciousness. This growing complexity involves not only a greater *number* of elements, and a greater *variety* of elements, but also a wider range and variety of *connections* between them. The sponge, for example, has a low complexity. It consists of many similar cells with no nervous system and having only stereotyped relationships. It is capable of very limited response to its environment. The earthworm, more complex, has a number of almost identical segments each with its nerve centre, but these have very little connection even with neighbouring segments. Its behaviour is simple and stereotyped. The octopus, by contrast, with its large central brain, has complex connections throughout its whole body. It is capable of much more flexible behaviour. The bees in a hive demonstrate the same principle in a collective form. The individual worker bees are more or less identical, and communications between them, though remarkable, are again simple and stereotyped. The behaviour of the hive and of its individual inmates is, at any rate by human standards, very inflexible, for though it has a greater number of elements, there is no corresponding increase in variety. It would thus appear that this growing complexity in living things, requiring both division of labour and also variety of communication, leads to flexibility of response. It opens up the possibility of greater freedom.

The complexity of a city, too, may often seem to be like that of a sponge, an earthworm, an octopus or a hive of bees. But to envisage its true complexity we have to move beyond the consideration of any single animal, or even of the beehive and the anthill. We have, first, to consider ecology—the balance of nature—the harmonious interaction of animal, vegetable and mineral, by which each element is dependent upon and contributes to the whole environment. The ecology (or ekistics) of the city involves the total harmony of man with nature, with his fellow-men, with his own buildings and networks. But secondly, within this total ecology, the city is no beehive or anthill, for its true complexity involves the co-operation and communication of millions of human beings, each one different from every other, but participating together and supplying each other's needs. If complexity is the principle of the evolution of life, then the next advance in evolution would seem to be such a community of men, women and children, living in ordered complexity with each other, with nature and with their own man-made environment, and opening up for each other the possibility of a more abundant life and of greater freedom.

This advance is difficult to achieve. Complexity requires of every person that he shall become more perfectly and uniquely himself, while at the same time subordinating his aggressive instinct to the wellbeing of the community. It also demands a new quality of leadership. It requires of us all that we enter into the freedom which it offers, through obedience to authority—but this authority must be exercised by leaders who are encouraging us to participate, and who are promoting not themselves but the on-going principle of evolution and of life. Any sane man would willingly co-operate with evolution —and in the end we can only realize our freedom by abandoning ourselves to our destiny. Such changes only come about under the catastrophic and creative impact of a common threat and a common hope. The threat to our modern cities is increasingly clear to us all, and it is set out with authority in the following chapters. But with equal clarity and authority there emerges from the words of these five wise men a hope and a way forward. The hope is complexity, in its fullest meaning of embracing one another. We must cry complexity—participation— love—till men catch the vision. We must experiment with it in action till we see that it is both the process towards the goal and the goal itself. Till we understand together that it is both the way and the truth and the life. Till we learn to embrace embracing—to love love. ...

Till, in the end, complexity becomes simplicity, and the engineer is one with the artist.

Have you ever thought, not only about the aeroplane but about whatever man builds, that all of man's industrial efforts, all his computations and calculations, all the nights spent over working draughts and blueprints, invariably culminate in the production of a thing whose sole and guiding principle is the ultimate of simplicity?

It is as if there were a natural law which ordained that to achieve this end, to refine the curve of a piece of furniture, or a ship's keel, or the fuselage of the aeroplane, until gradually it partakes of the elementary purity of the curve of a human breast or shoulder, there must be the experimentation of several generations of craftsmen. In anything at all, perfection is finally attained not when there is no longer anything to add but when there is no longer anything to take away, when the body has been stripped down to its nakedness.

It results from this that perfection of invention touches hands with absence of invention, as if that line which the human eye will follow with effortless delight were a line that had not been invented but simply discovered, had in the beginning been hidden by nature and in the end been found by the engineer. There is an ancient myth about the image asleep in the block of marble until it is carefully disengaged by the sculptor. The sculptor must himself feel that he is not so much inventing or shaping the curve of a breast or shoulder as delivering the image from its prison.[1]

[1] *Wind, Sand and Stars* by Antoine de Saint-Exupéry, William Heinemann, p. 53; Penguin Books 1966, p. 40.

1. Living in Cities

COLIN BUCHANAN

Professor of Transport, Imperial College, London

THE FORCE which has drawn us together this week has been a compelling anxiety about the conditions arising in urban areas all over the world, the areas into which more and more people are being steadily born or drawn. Last year I visited Calcutta. I was driven in from the airport in the late evening. I noticed many sacks lying about on the sidewalks, in porches and under arcades. Upon inquiry I learned that these were not sacks, but homeless people sleeping where they could, wrapped up in thin blankets. I saw the slightly better off people who had managed to set themselves up with flimsy shelters. I saw the 'bustees'—huge shanty towns with open sewers in the streets and vast middens of refuse. I saw the buses overcrowded to the point that people were hanging on to the outside wherever they could get a grip, sometimes falling off, sometimes being swept off or crushed by another vehicle. Calcutta gave me the feeling of something very frightening indeed—a huge urban area on the point of breakdown.

I have been to São Paulo in Brazil—a great, lusty, sprawling, powerful place, where the central skyscrapers grow in riotous confusion, and the suburbs push farther and farther out every day. So rapid is the growth that the provision of services lags far behind. I was told that 40 per cent of the population do not have a garbage collection, and the percentage is tending to increase. I heard of cases where poor people had to spend three hours travelling to work in the morning, and three hours back again at night. The traffic was beyond anything I have seen in any city I have visited.

I have seen the slums and the ghettos in the United States—in New York, in Detroit, in Chicago and in Los Angeles. I have seen people living at 2,000 persons per acre in Hong Kong, where, if you stand in the courtyards of the vast tenement blocks, the accumulation of thousands of ordinary conversations comes out of the building like a dull roar. I know the cities of Britain pretty well. I know their slums. I know their schemes of redevelopment, some of which I admire, some of which cause me to wonder deeply. I am aware of the interminable arguments that go on about government, administration, finance and control, green belts and sprawl, public and private transport.

I am convinced that, after the fundamental question of preserving peace, it is the form and organization of urban areas that is now looming up as the greatest social challenge for the world for the rest of this century.

So far I have deliberately avoided the use of the word 'cities'. The trouble with the word 'city' is that it means different things to different people. In England it still tends to be mixed up with places that have cathedrals or old charters. In the U.S.A. some very small places have somehow got themselves the title of 'city'. In other cases the term 'central city' is applied to the administrative nucleus of some gigantic sprawling megalopolis. Also the term 'city' has a romantic connotation for many people—

a place of dreaming towers and spires, which may be a very un-useful vision for the future. So I prefer to use the prosaic term 'urban area', which can cover everything from a village to that vast sprawl on the eastern seaboard of the U.S.A. where it is impossible to see on the ground where one 'city' ends and the next begins.

Why, if urban areas are as troublesome as I have indicated, should we have them at all? The answer is that it is the way of the world. The population of the world has increased enormously since the discovery of power and the industrial revolution. To keep this huge population supplied with all the things it needs requires many activities. For the most part these activities may have to be conducted in buildings, and between the buildings (as between dwellings and factories, for example) all kinds of relationships develop. Once buildings are set in relation to other buildings you get, by my definition, an urban area. The development of industry and commerce—which seems to be the only way the people of the world can advance themselves beyond the subsistence level—inevitably connotes urbanization. I do not think there is any escape from this. In the so-called 'advanced countries' the bulk of the population is already concentrated in urban areas, and in the developing countries people are on the move into urban areas. This urban migration does not necessarily signify any loss of agricultural production. Some land, it is true, has to be used for urban purposes, but otherwise the lesson is the same from all countries—major increases of agricultural production can be achieved with fewer and fewer people. So, far from urbanization being detrimental to agriculture, the improvement of agriculture is a cause of the drift to urban areas.

Thus an urban area is a complex of linked buildings. The buildings are of many types, and many of them are extremely complicated in themselves. A teaching hospital, for example, is so complex that it can take twelve years to design and build. The linkages between buildings are of many kinds. There are pipes, ducts and wires which enable substances, ideas, and information to flow from building to building; and there are roads and railways which enable people and commodities to move around. This brings me to the second stage of my definition of an urban area. It is only partly correct to say that an urban area is a complex of linked buildings—it is also a complex occupied by people. Between the people and the buildings there is constant interaction. Very few people are able to occupy a building purpose-designed for their needs; in the main it is a matter of people adapting buildings to their needs and adapting their needs to the buildings available. So urban areas are constantly changing—the buildings change, people come and go, they do different things. The people and the buildings mould each other. Some buildings come to be loved, some to be hated. Some buildings depress and impoverish people, others provide people with opportunities. An urban area is the strangest mixture of effect and counter-effect, the scene of extraordinary associations between people and inanimate artifacts.

So I come to the third stage of my definition. An urban area is an assemblage of linked buildings occupied by people *who are engaged in a great variety of interdependent activities*. An ordinary family is dependent on office or factory for its income, on schools for the education of its children, on hospitals when sickness comes, on shops for the everyday things of life. All manner of interconnected systems are at work—the education system, the postal system, the employment system, the retailing system, the transport system, and so on.

Do not be misled by vague concepts that the city is the

church, or the aspiration of the people, or the spiritual home, or the citadel of culture or anything like that. A city is an urban area, an agglomeration of buildings made and occupied by man for his own practical purposes. The only way in which we can hope to get the better of urban problems is to strive for more knowledge and better understanding of what goes on in urban areas and how they work. The functioning of urban areas is infinitely more complicated than most people have been willing to admit. The problems are partly human and partly material.

Lest anyone should think I am generalizing too much, I would like to emphasize the similarity of urban areas the world over. They may differ in detail—one may be inland and another coastal, one may be a commercial centre, another a steel town, and a third a holiday resort —but they all provide shelter for people of very much the same shape, size, habits and needs. It is, after all, this broad similarity which has brought people of all nationalities to this conference; and it is this broad similarity which suggests to me the possibilities and advantages of international studies of urban problems.

I would like to proceed now to set out my own list of the twelve most crucial problems or groups of problems which seem to be arising in urban areas. I have tried to restrict my list to what might be called 'first-order' problems; that is to say, defective situations actually present in virtually all sizeable urban areas. I have not concerned myself with 'second-order' problems, by which I mean the problems of solving problems—the problem, for example, or organizing the construction industry in order to solve the housing problem.

I have set out first the problems which I feel sure about. They are material problems which I *know* exist, and could if necessary substantiate. At the end of the list I set down two problems which I *think* exist; they are based on subjective judgements of my own and of other people, but I have very little scientific data that I can bring in support.

1. The sheer shortage of accommodation for many purposes. The most distressing examples arise in rapidly growing areas in the form of shortage of dwellings. In many cases the urban explosion, arising from natural increase, from the inward migrations from de-populating rural areas and perhaps as a result of famine or persecution, is posing housing problems of terrible severity. The situation carries with it the risk that in the desperate need to get something done in a hurry, decisions will be taken which are not in the best long-term interests of the area.

2. Physical problems connected with the existing buildings. Many are old, decayed, out of date, inconvenient, or have unacceptable standards of sanitation, daylight, aspect, surrounding space or garbage disposal. These defects can be found in all classes of buildings—dwellings, offices, factories, schools, hospitals, etc.—and they have consequential effects on the activities within the buildings.

3. Disagreeable environments in the sense of surroundings that are drab, dirty, uninteresting and as likely as not beset with dangers and nuisances arising from motor traffic.

4. Difficulties of movement for people and goods. Most urban areas the world over have grown 'naturally' as a result of the play of market forces without anyone giving much thought to the problems of movement as they gradually build up. Especially awkward are the problems

arising from the wide dispersal of low-density suburban housing estates coupled with increasing concentrations of commercial activities at urban centres. The journey-to-work problems that result are only too obvious.

5. Pollution—a range of questions concerned with water and atmospheric pollution and the disposal of waste products of all kinds. Some urban areas are growing so rapidly that garbage collection and drainage cannot keep pace.

6. Inadequacies in various social services—lack of medical facilities, poor education services, inhuman conditions for old people, etc. Some of these may be associated with defective buildings or lack of buildings, or they may be the result of shortage of manpower.

7. Defects in the economic base—instability, lack of employment opportunities in sufficient variety, etc.—leading to dissatisfaction, unemployment and possibly poverty. Under this heading there can be the strange contradiction of poverty existing in a society which over-all is far from poor.

8. Maintenance of law and order—a range of problems aggravated by the tendency for criminals to collect in crowded areas where the pickings are to be had.

9. Lack of worthwhile things for people of all ages to do with their leisure time.

10. A complex range of questions concerned with the government, administration and financing of urban areas. These tend to be aggravated as urban areas expand and coalesce, when new problems arise which transcend the boundaries of local authorities and, as a result, are nobody's responsibility to handle. Under this heading

come the problems of 'regionalism'.

11. A wide range of human problems. Here I find myself on much less certain ground. Some of these are involved with matters already mentioned—unemployment and the unhappiness caused by bad housing or lack of housing. These I recognize as problems, as I can recognize loneliness and poverty. But my hunch is that there are many others where documentation has scarcely begun. I guess, for example, that many people in urban areas suffer from a 'sense of entrapment'—they are caught in conditions from which they cannot escape; they are tyrannized by public decisions; they live in rigid surroundings where there is no freedom of action: no freedom to bang about, no freedom to start an enterprise, no freedom for a man to express himself even to the extent of painting his front door the colour he wants. Everything is rule-ridden. I *think* this is the case, but I have no data to prove it.

12. The final item is not so much another problem as a complication of the whole. It is the additional complicating overlay that pervades all the previous problems, arising out of questions of race, religion, ideology or history. Some problems, for example, are bad enough when there is only one racial group involved; when several are concerned they become fiendishly difficult.

I have thought it necessary to put before you a provisional list of problems because I believe this is the only possible way to make progress. In the last few years I must have listened to thousands of hours of discussion about urban problems—much of it futile because it has been about problems which have never been defined, even roughly. I doubt whether any of the problems I have set out really have solutions in any concise sense of the term—they are more in the nature of situations which can be dealt with only by policies patiently applied over long periods—but this does not detract from the need to identify the problem areas as the prelude to policy making and the settling of priorities.

There does not seem to be any way of tackling these urban problems other than by the process we loosely call 'planning'. This means giving some organization the authority to control the course of development and re-development—to say where new dwellings, new industries, new roads and so on should be put and in what quantities, with the object of preventing the whole place getting into muddle and confusion. This sounds simple, but in fact to set up a planning system in a country is a slow and formidable business. It involves legislation and the surrender of certain rights. In quite a real sense, a community has to be ready to receive planning. Britain probably has the most sophisticated and onerous planning system of any country in the world, but it has taken sixty years to build it up, and it has probably come about only because the pressures of population in such a small island have pointed the need for the control of development in a fairly obvious way.

At this conference I have heard it complained that planning has failed in this or that respect in some country, but I have known that in that country there is really no planning system worthy of the name. There are no powers, no properly constituted planning authorities, and very few professional staff. Planning has not really started.

There is no alternative to planning. The appalling results of allowing development to run its own way governed only by market forces can be seen all over the world. What each country must do is to strive to develop its planning system, gathering the financial, legal and intellectual resources that are needed, and seeking to make the system ever more effective, constructive and humane. I am sure that *this* is the really important message which the delegates to the conference should take back to their countries. *Develop your planning systems.* It is a prosaic message, but I think it is fundamental. Unless there is a planning machine in which people can participate, then talk of participation is futile.

However, most institutions improve themselves as a result of criticisms, and what has emerged from this conference, above everything else, is a sense of considerable anxiety that in the work of planning quite insufficient attention has been paid to human needs and values, and that people have been or are being denied the right to participate in decisions affecting their own lives. This is a serious criticism and I think it is right that I should devote the rest of this address to a consideration of it.

I can, of course, speak with knowledge only of the conditions in my own country, Britain. But we have been through the mill in this country, and there is a great deal in our experience which is of general application. On the first point—that insufficient attention has been paid to human needs—I think I would be prepared as a professional planner to accept the criticism. For example, in the field in which I am particularly interested, namely motor traffic, it is only in the last few years that the anti-environmental effects of motor traffic—the dangers, anxieties, noise, pollution, visual confusion and so on—have been put together and seen for what they really are—a major social problem. Yet planners have had traffic problems on their plates for nearly sixty years. In housing, in shopping, in office design, in the problems of getting people to work and children to school, in the adjustment problems when people are shifted from slum areas to new towns—in these and other matters far too little attention has been paid to all the subtleties of human needs and aspirations. Too often it has been left to hard-pressed social workers to deal with the human problems as best they can after the main decisions have been implemented. The lesson of the last twenty years has been that even when the big decisions *are* right a great deal can go horribly wrong with the details. It is no comfort to the husband of a young wife who is driven to suicide by loneliness, to be told that the broad plan and location of the new town cannot be faulted.

I could of course cite arguments in defence of the professional planners and architects. Too often they have had to act as their own amateur sociologists owing to some strange reluctance (as it has seemed to me) of the sociologists to join in. I think this is being put right now. Then again, the professionals are not the decision makers. They only recommend, and very very often they have to watch in silence as their recommendations are thwarted, or pared away.

But when all is said and done, I would admit that much more work needs to be done on the study of human needs and aspirations. It should cover not only present human needs, but future needs as well. Let me give one example. In this tight little country of Britain it is reasonable to suppose (unless some disaster overtakes us) that there will be a steady rise of incomes, that people will have more leisure, and that they will gradually become better educated. What is going to be the effect of this, in particular on residential areas where people spend most of their time and which are by far the largest users of urban land? At the moment a man comes home from work, dog tired, to a little flat on the twentieth floor of some block.

He watches the telly, sleeps, and gets off to work early next morning. But what will happen when he has to spend perhaps four days a week at home? What will he do with himself? It is an important question because men get dangerous when they are bored. Am I right in thinking that as incomes and expectations rise there will be an inexorable demand for more spacious living conditions which provide more opportunities for people to do things that interest them?

I turn now to the second criticism, that people are not being given the chance to participate in the decisions that affect their lives. I find this a very difficult matter. I imagine, for example, that the demand for participation arises from the fact that the decisions are proving faulty in some way. But if the decisions were right, and everyone was happy, then would the demand for participation still have arisen? I doubt it. It is only when the train service goes abominably wrong that the ticket holders rise in their wrath and demand, if not a say in the organization, at any rate the right to express their requirements. So I really am inclined to divert some of the demand for participation by saying that it could be met if the planning was itself much better, based on better information, better researches, better knowledge of human needs, thus leading to better-quality decisions.

Two other considerations reinforce this view. The first is that decision making is tending to become a more and more sophisticated process, moving, if anything, further away from the people. New methods of decision making are being developed—questions are being considered on much wider fronts, the costs and benefits of alternative courses of action have to be assessed, the possible consequences of policies considered, and the consequences of those consequences, and so on. We seem to be standing at the dramatic moment when the techniques of operational research and systems analysis, which have yielded remarkable results in commerce and industry, are about to be applied to social questions. The tendency, then, seems to be to shift the decision-making process farther from public participation and even from public comprehension.

The second consideration is the question of changing values. This is a reflection of the point I made earlier about the need to consider the development of human desires in the future. So many planning decisions are made not for today but for tomorrow. Who is to participate in the decisions for tomorrrow? Who is to participate in the decisions (required today) relating to the planning of a new town which will be occupied in the first instance by youngsters now at school? How do we know what their values will be, and if we were to seek them, would they be reliable? These few days in Coventry have made me think a lot about the young people, because the place seems to be chock full of them. What *are* their values? On Saturday evening I walked past the window of Owen Owen facing Broadgate Square by the bus stops. I counted twenty couples, the girls perched on the convenient rail of the curved non-reflecting windows, and the young men pressed up against them, seemingly happy to be in the public view, indifferent to the litter of the day all around them on the pavement. Privacy is certainly not one of their values. On Sunday I sat for a while in the old cathedral. A young couple came in and the girl burst out with a laugh saying, 'What is it all in aid of?', and from the way she looked round I am sure she wasn't just referring to the sculpture exhibits. What is it in aid of? Twenty-five years ago the decision was taken to preserve the ruin of the old cathedral. To those of us who lived through the 1940s it is still a searing, tearing place. I do not know who participated in the decision at the time, but I do know that the bold-as-brass youngsters I see in Broadgate Square had nothing to do with it. It really would not surprise me, and I should have some sympathy with them, if one day they rose up and said, 'This is a living city, what do we want with this burned out hulk in the middle of it?'

However, having said all that, I admit once again that far more could and should be done in the administration of planning to allow people to participate in the decisions that affect them. I suspect that the matters in which people want to participate are really quite ordinary matters. They are not the great strategic issues but the everyday concerns of ordinary folk. The trouble with planning is that it tends to concentrate on the strategic issues and fails to develop the delicate tendrils that are needed to sense out the local personal problems. I accept this. I also accept that even where participation is not possible, in the direct sense, there is an obligation on planners to consult and to explain. This is especially necessary in view of the tendency for decision making to become more and more the end product of highly complicated analytical techniques.

So, if I might attempt to summarize:

1. Urbanization seems to be the inexorable tendency all over the world.
2. It is giving rise to grave problems of the utmost relevance to human welfare. This may not be apparent to someone who has a nice house and a garden in the English countryside, but this country has its urban problems as desperate in their way as those of any other place.
3. Basically the only way in which these problems can be tackled is by the development of more effective planning systems and institutions. This

is the rather matter-of-fact message which the delegates to the conference must take home for their countries above all else. But, of course, in order to develop institutions, it is necessary to demonstrate why they are needed and what they can achieve. This is where the delegates must act as missionaries.

4. In the development of planning institutions it is necessary to combine two approaches. First, the problems must be treated for what they are— highly complicated, difficult, interlinked questions deserving of the scientific approach in the full sense of the term with the application of the best techniques available. Second, the problems must be treated for what they are—deeply involved at every turn with human beings of every description, the wayward, the irrational, the bold, the frightened, the young, the old, the healthy and the sick. These are the clients of planning. Without understanding of their needs planning cannot succeed. This is the approach of compassion, and this, as I see it, is where the Christian church has a major role to play.

2. Community and Communication

What are Cities and what are they for?

BY

RICHARD HARE

Professor of Moral Philosophy, University of Oxford

IF WE ASK, in Socratic fashion, 'What is a city?', it is tempting to answer, in the fashion of Le Corbusier, 'A city is a machine for *communicating* in.' But 'machine' would be wrong. A city is not a machine. It is not normally designed; it grows. Often you cannot stop it growing. When things go wrong with cities, they are less like the breakdowns which affect machines than like the diseases which afflict animals and plants. The town planner is not like an engineer (he cannot *repair* a city like a motor-car); he is like a doctor looking after a living organism, which he keeps healthy if he can, or, if he cannot, tries to restore it to health—by surgery if he must. But even surgery is not like repairing a car; the organism has to grow well again after you have interfered with it. The car comes back from the garage as good as it was before the trouble started; when the man comes back from hospital it may be months before he is really well again.

Or we might say that town planning is like gardening. Even in the literal sense gardening is an important part of it—such as the landscape gardening of genius which has redeemed the mostly second-rate architecture of Canberra, and made it a fine city in spite of itself. But even when he is planting not trees but people, the town planner has, like the gardener, to plant and pray. How the thing that he has planted thrives, he can to some extent influence by the care he gives it; but it is largely out of his control. For all that, there are good and bad gardeners. The planner's contribution is important. He cannot leave everything to nature. As the old gardener said to his pious master, 'You ought to see what the garden gets like after God has had it to himself for a bit.' And there is an important difference between cities and gardens: plants, if badly looked after, just die; human beings protest and rebel. So you had better respect their feelings, if you want their co-operation.

Let us say, then, that a city is, not a machine, but an *organism for communication*. Why 'for communication'? Let us imagine a country whose inhabitants do not live in cities, or even in villages (which are a kind of small cities), but spread out in their houses at equal intervals all over the countryside. Of what would they be deprived? They can grow food and eat it, they can grow cotton and wool and clothe themselves, and they can build houses. They can also exploit such mineral resources as do not require the co-operation of large numbers of people to mine them. What will they *not* be able to do because they do not have cities or villages? The answer is that, generally speaking, they cannot communicate. There may be a postal service (but where did they learn to write?), or even a telephone service (but the telephone was invented and perfected in cities), or radio and television (whose stations, however, are nearly always centred on cities). But they cannot go and shop (shopping is one form of communication; its essence is an agreement to exchange money for goods, and to reach an agreement, we have to communicate). They cannot have a government (all forms of government, however tyrannical, are forms of communication; laws, for example, are pieces of language telling people what they have to do; and language is communication). That is why it is difficult to conceive of government without a seat of government—that is, a capital city. To govern, it is necessary for people to *come together* and talk to each other.

The reason why it is almost impossible to have either commerce or government without cities is that both are forms of communication, and communication of nearly all kinds involves people coming together, which they cannot do unless they have somewhere to come to. The same is true of the arts. The people in my imaginary country without cities would be extremely unlikely to develop any arts worth mentioning; nearly all arts depend on either a market or an audience, and you cannot have either of these things unless people come together. Art is a form of communication; it depends on there being people to communicate with. This applies especially to architecture. You are unlikely to get fine buildings put up in a city in which communications have broken down.

Commerce; government; art: all these kinds of communication largely depend on the existence of cities. But we need now to ask more precisely what we mean by 'communication'. It will at once become evident that we mean more than one thing. First of all there is communication in the crudest physical sense: the sense in which 'Communications' appears as one of the chapter headings in almost any city planner's report. The chapter is usually the one which excites the most controversy, and on it, usually, everything else in the plan depends. Physical communications are, indeed, a means, not an end; but they are an essential means if the city is to function. If shoppers find it too inconvenient to get to the shops, or if the shopkeepers find it too expensive to get their goods from the wholesaler or factory, the shopping centre declines. If members of parliament miss important votes because they are held up in traffic blocks, or if civil servants are late for committees of which they are essential members—or if, as in New Delhi, the clerks in the offices have to exhaust themselves every morning and evening bicycling for miles and miles up Lutyens' magnificent vistas, or, as in London, cram themselves into trains which cannot be relied on—government and commerce cannot function well. Nor can the arts, if you cannot be sure of arriving on time for a concert or a play.

This is not an argument for or against any particular mode of transport. There are many modes; but whatever modes are adopted, they must enable people to come into and travel within a city with reasonable convenience in order to communicate with one another—for that is what the city is for. And in so doing, they must not make it impossible for other people to do *their* communicating. These other people, too, live in communities, which must not be divided by streams of traffic; if they are, communication between one side of the street and the other will become dangerous, and there will be so much noise that verbal communication is difficult anywhere near the street.

But physical communication, or transport, is not an end in itself. When I am sitting by myself in my car, I am not communicating, but only trying to get somewhere in order to communicate with somebody. One of the chief difficulties facing those who govern cities is to decide the relative importance of the communication that different people are trying to achieve by coming into cities. Professor Buchanan stressed that, if we insist on a reasonable standard of environment in our cities (which means, at least, an environment which makes human communication easy), the amount of transport we can have coming in to and going out of them (the accessibility, as he calls it) will depend on what we can afford to spend, and in many cases will be limited even then. So we have to distinguish between essential and inessential traffic. And this means distinguishing between those whose journeys are really necessary and those whose journeys are not. But how can we do this without an assessment of the importance of the communication which is the object of the journey? Who is to make this value judgement? Here are two people stuck in two different traffic jams going into the same city centre to meet one another: how important is it that they should succeed?

The bigger a city is, the more intractable these problems become, as has been shown mathematically by the work of Professor Smeed and others. This has led to the demand that we should limit the size of cities—if only we could! Probably the most helpful approach is to ask what forms of communication are essential to the life of a particular city as an organism for communication, and to offer the other forms incentives to transfer elsewhere. For example, in London and other big cities many firms have moved their main offices to the suburbs; and the same thing has happened to shopping centres in many places. The proposal has even been made to move the seat of government of this country to Yorkshire. It is obvious that if the federal capital of the United States had been in New York, the problems of that city would have been even more difficult than they are. To move a seat of government may be intended not merely to ease the traffic problems in the city it leaves, but to improve communications with the region it goes to, as in the case of Brazilia. To some extent, cities can specialize with respect to the kind of communication that goes on in them.

And not only cities, but also the parts of cities. What planners call 'zoning' is a useful device for achieving such specialization; it means that you limit the forms of communication that are allowed to take place (devoting an area, for example, to a shopping centre, or to a university), in order to make that kind of communication convenient, and to prevent it (or the traffic it generates) interfering with other kinds of communication. Or the total amount of *any* kind of communication that is allowed to take place in a given area can be limited. A wise man in the planning department of Canberra (he was, I think, a disciple of Professor Doxiadis) said to me, 'When we are planning an area, we work out how much the roads will carry, and we don't allow more building and more activities to take place in the area than will generate that amount of traffic.' If this rule had been followed in all cities (it has had lip-service paid to it in many) how much happier they would be!

But once one starts to zone a city—or once it starts zoning itself naturally, as often happens—a great danger emerges. The price of specialization is isolation. In making it easy for members of parliament to communicate with members of parliament, or businessmen with businessmen, we make it more difficult for them to communicate with other sorts of people. If cities get too segregated —one area for the rich, another for the poor, one for government, another for the governed—then, certainly, communication between one rich man and another rich man, or between one member of the governing class and another member of the governing class, will become much easier. And so, for that matter, will be that between one poor man and another in the same poor district. But the rich and the governing class will be talking to one another in a language which the poor do not understand, and the poor will be talking to each other—perhaps talking of revolution—in a language which (terrifyingly) their rulers do not understand.

We must not forget that a city—an organism for communication—has to be a community. A community is a group of people who can communicate with each other. The city, if it is functioning properly, is something which all of them have *in common*. It is *their* city, and the government of the city is in communication with the people who are being governed. If this communication is cut off, then nobody should be surprised if, in order to re-establish it—to make themselves heard—the governed resort to violence. That, at least, gets them into the newspapers, which their rulers read; so communication is to that extent re-established. Often the rulers, fearing violence, provoke or even start it; for they too have lost the ability to communicate in any other way with those whom they are trying to govern. A community in which violence is the only channel of communication between the ruled and the rulers is a very unhappy one. But it is happier than if there were no communication at all. If Washington were an all-white city, the United States would be worse governed.

How can communication be re-established or preserved otherwise than by violence? How can the city be made into a community? Success in communication is making oneself understood, and understanding what the other person is saying. The instrument of communication is language, and this is what we have to learn. It is much easier now than it was, to *hear* what other people are saying, because of the so-called mass-communication media (the press and radio and television). We *hear* each other by means of communications satellites. But do we always *understand* one another? Do we know each others' languages? Does the Englishman, or the American understand what the Hindi speaker is trying to say to him, even when it is translated into English? The mass media can help us to understand, because if one goes on talking, and talking in the right way (argument and explanation, not rhetoric and propaganda), and if, more important still, one goes on listening, one may in the end learn the other person's language. We are beginning to conquer illiteracy. If people can read, they may begin to understand; and even if they cannot read, they may understand what they hear on the radio. But if those who control the radio are trying, for example, to stop the Arabs understanding the Israelis, it might be better if there were no radio at all. The right motto for those in charge of these means of communication is, 'Nation shall speak peace unto nation'. The 'nations' may be those which share and divide a single country or city—rich and poor, black and white. And one cannot speak peace without learning to understand the language of peace.

The key to successful communication, in cities as elsewhere, is understanding; and the key to understanding is education. Education means, or at least always involves, learning to understand a language—for example, the language of mathematics, of science, of democratic politics. Once the language is understood, there is little more to be learnt. The discipline which has as its task the furthering of this understanding is called philosophy; it seeks out the most difficult concepts in our language—the ones which tie us into the biggest knots—and tries to elucidate them so that the knots can be unravelled. The job of philosophy is the clarification of what is obscure in language (little as you would think it, to hear some philosophers talk). A philosopher can perhaps make a small, but essential, contribution to the success of our conference, by beginning the elucidation of what is sure to be its central theme: communication. The conference will be successful to the extent that we manage to communicate with one another about communication between people and cities.

POSTSCRIPT[1]

What then is this language of peace which we have to understand if we are to live at peace in cities? It is the language of morality, and the language of love. To think that love and morality have different languages, so that the one can be at variance with the other, is a mistake often made by those to whom love means sex, and morality means a book of rules the reasons for which everyone has forgotten. But in truth morality *is* love. For the essence of morality is to treat the interests of others as of equal weight with one's own. Its supreme principle, as Bentham saw, is that everybody is to count as one and nobody as more than one. This means that in making moral decisions we have always to say to ourselves:

> *Momentous to himself as I to me*
> *Is every man that ever woman bore.*

Only so shall we be able, as Kant put it, to will the maxim of our action to be universal law. But this is also the rule of love, that as we wish that men should do to us, so we should do to them. This is what it is to love our neighbour as ourself.

In the modern city, hate between rich and poor, rulers and ruled, is much easier to preach than love; but unless love is both preached and most skilfully practised, our cities will fall apart.

[1] This was added after the conference.

3. People and Cities

BY

CONSTANTINE DOXIADIS

Director of the Institute of Ekistics, Athens

WE ARE bewildered today by the problems of people and cities because we forget that five different elements are involved:

nature;
man as an individual;
society;
shells (buildings of all kinds);
networks (from roads to telecommunications).

These can be seen from five different angles:

economic;
social;
political;
technological;
cultural.

In combination, there are not, as may appear, twenty-five types of problem, but more than 33 million. Each individual has his own attitude towards the city and is aware of a different problem. In a free society, the problem of people and cities is more complex than any other facing humanity. That is why we need to establish a systematic approach. Let us look at this issue under three aspects: the crisis, the challenge and the response.

Our cities are facing an unprecedented crisis. Up to three centuries ago, cities were small and static. With the revolutions in science, technology and industry, the situation changed and soon got out of control. Growth and decay in cities accentuated social divisions. The absence of exact statistics does not allow us to say that crime occurs more often in large cities than in small ones, but it is a fact that more and more young people are becoming criminals.

The crisis in our buildings is seen in the increase in squatters and slum dwellers and in the number of those who draw their curtains to shut out the parking lots. The crisis in networks means that we cross our big cities at a slower speed than people were able to at the beginning of the century in horse-drawn carts. Many people say that man will adapt himself to this new situation. Is it desirable that he should?

In the city, stresses multiply. The city of the past had its own scale, with things in proportion and for convenience. Today, multi-storey buildings are changing the scale of the city and complicating the transportation.

We do not know how to cope with these and other urban problems. When I was presenting the plans for the new city of Rio de Janeiro two years ago, I was asked one of the most searching questions ever put to me: 'Mr Doxiadis, when we finish eliminating the slums, who is going to compose the samba, who is going to compose our music?' I could not answer this question. Until we can answer it, we shall not understand our cities, because we do not know how and where man expresses himself.

We still look backwards like Homeric man, not looking

to the future as we believe we do now, but looking into the past as he did with back turned to the frightening future. Because we can build multi-storey buildings, we create a city in many respects more dangerous than the tower of Babel. The tower of Babel could not be finished, but a modern city can, and this can lead us to disaster.

Because of our failure with cities, we escape in several ways. We escape to the outskirts, and we escape to the 'Utopia' of the small city. The only two people in our generation who had the imagination and courage to offer specific proposals for a better city, Aldous Huxley and Professor Skinner, proposed very small cities below 1,000 people. They forgot that we shall never have advanced services if there are only small cities, since such things as cars and medical research are the products of the very large city.

Some say that we shall build better cities when we have regional government, but this evades the real problems. We are in a crisis of cities; and we cannot think that by recognizing this crisis, we have done something to solve it. The crisis today is as nothing in relation to the one we shall have to face tomorrow.

THE CHALLENGE

The real challenge, then, is not what has happened, what is happening, but what can happen. We must face the future realistically. For instance, we must be aware of the biological forces that are operating. Should we try to control these? Even if birth control becomes general, there will be on this earth 12,000 million people by the middle of the next century. This will produce problems not just four times greater than today's, but ten times greater, because the present 1,000 million urban dwellers will then have grown into 10,000 million urban dwellers. So our cities will have, on the average, ten times more citizens—

and, as people now use more land *per capita,* these cities are going to be at least forty times larger than now.

As technology is developing, the forces in these cities will be huge. The distances between our cities are rapidly diminishing. We are already building great urban systems that will soon lead to a universal city of man, the ecumenopolis, in which all cities are interconnected. This phenomenon is completely unavoidable so long as we believe in individual freedom and development. Is it reasonable to try to avoid the immense city because it may crush man to death? We can only know that such a city must create a very great danger for us because it is extra-human in dimension and it is becoming inhuman in content. We are in peril, in the future, of turning the city of man into a necropolis, a dead city.

We cannot change the evolution of history. Probably biologists will tell us that the forces which decide our fate today have developed over billions of years. But that is no reason why, if we understand these forces properly and our own ability to deal with them, and if we develop some wisdom, we should not find a better road to follow by acting like the Chinese gardener who, before sunrise, massages the new branches of his tree to give them a better shape.

What we need is a human scale, within an extra-human, an inhuman frame. Is this reasonable? I will only remind you that most of you came here by using jet planes which are inhuman machines within which we have created a human environment. This is what, through the exercise of reason and imagination, we must do for our cities. Within the universal city of man, in order to survive, we must learn to create human cells. We have lost values by letting the cities of the past grow out of control. But we now understand that there are certain values expressed in the smaller dimensions of the cities of the past. These units are derived from human dimensions, from the child, the walking man, the seeing, the feeling, man. We have to understand that, as in nature, all organs of cities must grow by the repetition of cells. We have now to let our cities grow by human cells. What about the big city, then? If we commit ourselves to the small cells, to the small unit, what are we going to do about the big scale? Are we going to abandon life on the big scale? No. We must learn that life in the future will be life at different scales, for different age-groups, for different stages of our development.

We cannot make an absolute choice between the local neighbourhood and the city-wide community. We need a system of communities from the smallest to the largest —even if we have to go down below the community to the family and below the family to the individual, and in this way create a whole new scale within which we have to find ourselves. The question of local government versus regional government is not really relevant because even the local government factor is so complex. Can we really speak about local government in a city like New York with 10 million people? We must break down the very large units we have created into small communities to allow each one of us to find his position for every expression of his life. If we do this, we will allow for local participation in a systematic way at all levels. It is wrong to think of the old city limits only. It is wrong to think that there is only one answer to this difficult problem. We have to give several answers.

After travelling round the world and seeing people living in many cities, I believe that one of the answers to some of the problems is home ownership; that we must try to make most, if not all, of the people into home owners. In this universal city, we must also learn to respect not only universal but also local characteristics.

Our real goal should be the city of all men that will guarantee happiness and safety to us all.

THE RESPONSE

Can we achieve this? There is no magic formula and I can answer only on the basis of the experience I have gained. Are there any hopes beyond the hopes derived from Aeschylus who said that 'wisdom cometh from suffering'? Still, I do not think we should be pessimistic. Can we realize our dreams? When I ask this question, I remember something said by Senator Robert Kennedy: 'Some men see things as they are and say, why. I dream of things that never were and say, why not.'

First, do we have the financial resources to build a better city for man? The problem is not one of finance. Humanity as a whole is going to build from now to the end of the century more than it has ever built since the beginning of civilization. We are going to build, we are going to have much higher incomes, we are going to have much greater surpluses. The question is how to use them. How shall we employ them more wisely for all of us, for those who have, and for those who have not?

Secondly, if we have the financial resources to build, have we the space to build? All our projections show that there will be few problems of space for several generations to come. Problems will arise one century from now, but by then probably the population will begin to level off, because of many factors, social, biological, economic and political.

So we come to the third question. Do we have the human resources? Do we have the minds sufficiently able to make this immense city human? We will have no difficulty if we remember that we are now training throughout the world thousands more people than were trained a century ago. It has been calculated that 90 per cent of the scientific minds that have ever existed on this earth since the beginning of history are at present alive. Computers now allow us to calculate at a speed of one million times faster than man's natural calculating speed. If we now think of how many more trained people we have, and how much more quickly we can calculate, we see that we have the technical resources to tackle these difficult problems. There is therefore no physical reason why we should not build a proper city for men.

Who is going to do it? is the next question. The answer is, all of us. The city does not belong to any special group of experts. We must mobilize all our resources and all age-groups, from the artists to the political leaders, including the rebellious students. The gap has been widened between the decision makers and the young people. And this is one reason why we face such a critical situation. We don't communicate with the young any more. But we need them, including the post-war generation, which includes a wide spectrum from artists like the Beatles to politicians like Robert Kennedy, the generation which did not fight a Second World War, but which is entitled to fight with us for a better city.

How, then, are we going to achieve this great task? First, by refusing to adapt to the cities and by forcing the cities to adapt to us. Secondly, by again having the courage to dream with reason, which means learning from the past. Thirdly, by asking why, and by developing a systematic approach which can be the only basis on which we can achieve communication between all of us; and finally, by organizing our own cities properly. It is not the structure that creates problems, but our small minds, and our inability to understand that our future lies in better organization, better society and better and stricter structure of our cities. We have to understand that we are planning for huge areas defined not by our small minds but by people moving in space, who define the real forces in the city. We also have to understand that next to the proper scale of space, we have to select the proper scale of time. We feel proud when we have twenty-five-year plans, but we forget that our cities consist of all sorts of elements which live an average life of seventy years, people and buildings. We try to create the system by five- and ten-year plans, when we need plans extending from 100 to 150 years.

We must have the courage to plan for the cities to come, the cities, which only if conceived in this way will lead to the proper development of man through the proper development of the city. We need programmes for the growth of our cities and for change, and programmes of therapy for the suffering parts. If we lose our nerve and think that it should all happen tomorrow, we shall fail. We can say, 'In the fifties, we were still blind, and in the sixties our eyes were opened.' This may be the only big step we have made in the sixties, but it is a most important step. By the year 2000, when a conference on people and cities is again convened in this cathedral, then the speakers, those who today are young students at school or university, should be able to make the statement that man is in control again.

Are we going to do it?
Why not?

4. The Invisible Community

BY

RICHARD HAUSER

Director of the Centre for Group Studies, London

OUR HYPOTHESIS is that the best-planned community project can only supply the basic requirements for daily existence, such as houses, centres, transport facilities, etc. The requirements for full living—as against mere daily existence—cannot be organized from on top; all official planners can do is to hinder or to enable that most important of all reality factors, human warmth, to develop.

Human warmth is the true criterion of a successful community, and it grows out of the people's solidarity and their joy in one another. Where neighbours, friends and relatives have had their ties broken up by unenlightened housing policy and circumstance, this security must be reproduced by timely preparation. Whole armies of professionals could not produce either the mutual security or the spirit of adventure which will make people detach themselves from their television screens to create a way of life of their own. Anyone who pretends that the professionals can organize neighbourhood or community life on behalf of the people is either a fool or an interested fool. If people are not themselves involved right from the start, in fact before the actual move, their houses will mushroom into housing areas but will never become communities.

THE INVISIBLE COMMUNITY

Within the visible framework of its houses, buildings and streets the community has a fourth dimension which we call the invisible community. It is made up of the people's human relationships; their common links and roots which stem from a common past experience and the common purpose towards which they strive together. In the past, generations went into producing the values and traditions which created this invisible community and guaranteed its continued survival; although living in very bad physical conditions, people could still endure the most serious hardship, persecution and deprivation without losing their identity or their faith in better times ahead, because they had human warmth on which to fall back.

Today's communities, however, go to pieces despite the most adequate physical environment, and the most elaborate welfare administration; they do so precisely because they are deprived of this single most important factor in the building of communities, human warmth. The invisible community which took generations to evolve now has to be produced in a matter of a few years. The undergrowth of the intimate cross-relationships which gave cohesion to social structure has been ploughed up by forced change. People who are strangers to each other, who have no common social purpose that they know of, who share little common background, find themselves suddenly dumped into an alien environment, planned and built by experts *for them*. Because of their total unpreparedness and frustration, and the insecurity which is bound to result from these, they withdraw even further from one another, dependent on, yet resentful of, the authoritarian policies of those who act for them. They do not even feel that it is in any way their responsibility to do something about what happens in their street, their block, their neighbourhood, their city; they do not believe they can contribute anything at all to the planning which concerns their own children. If conditions of life for themselves or for their children need to be improved, 'The Welfare will see to it.'

But human warmth cannot be bought. It cannot be legislated for. It cannot be made to grow artificially. It can only be *enabled*. But at present every circumstance seems to militate against it.

BREAKDOWN OF THE INVISIBLE COMMUNITY: SYMPTOMS AND CAUSES

1. If nine tenths of understanding is lived experience and one tenth is outside observation, it is clear that people moving into new towns or into new housing under urban renewal schemes do so with little or no understanding of what this is actually going to mean to them. They have had no chance to experience indirectly any of the crises inherent in the coming change. Since they have not been actually involved as a community in planning either the move, or the place they are moving to, they have no real vested interest in it *as a community*, and are therefore concerned only with what affects them immediately as individuals.

2. The chances are that they have no *extended family* unit on which to fall back, no network of grandparents, uncles, aunts and cousins whom they can safely depend on in a crisis. They therefore feel quite alone in the world; a truncated family of two parents and two or three children, unused to asserting themselves and getting organized for joint action, either within their own extended family group or in a community. They would not

know how to go about defining common goals, participating in decision making or planning final action.

3. The present school system takes little notice of the youngsters' needs. In view of the fact that tens of thousands of young people will be transferred into other areas as part of slum clearance ('urban renewal' is a false term since the life of the city is not renewed at all, but only the buildings), it is shameful that the school gives them no social education whatever and so leaves them totally unprepared for the dangers and difficulties ahead of them. Of course they are equally unprepared for the potential joys and creative opportunities that the move may bring.

4. Because of their lack of experience and their ignorance of handling human relations, the young find it very difficult to carry frustration when pressure of events mounts in their lives; they often resort either to violence, which they cannot control once it explodes, or to apathy, which they cannot overcome once it engulfs them.

5. Those who plan the physical aspects of new communities have with few exceptions no solidarity with those who will live in them. 'They are lucky to get any housing at all' seems to be the general feeling. Budgets are tightened to exclude the essential 'extras', and planners and architects stick dutifully to them.

6. The motor-car is now the chief member of the physical community. Nothing is too good to accommodate its requirements, whereas children count for little and suffer the curse of lack of stimulus.

7. The unenlightened paternalists who shape other people's lives naturally prefer to deal with unquestioningly dependent customers rather than with strong group representatives. Therefore, whether consciously or not, they keep the people uninformed, unorganized, and manipulate them into submission by laying down for them

conditions of life under which at best they can only vegetate.

8. The desperate housing shortage makes for emphasis on houses and a cynical neglect of people's social needs, as if one necessarily excluded the other. High-density living areas need social amenities greater in number, variety and effectiveness than do lower-density areas. The social segregation of large numbers of people, with whom other sections of the population feel no solidarity, is the cause of low morale, much distress and eventual breakdown. For man is a tribal animal; the extended family is the basic defensive unit which gives inner security to the individual member, young or old. Any time the family is hurt or uprooted as in times of war, of suppression, of industrial revolution, or of urban renewal, every child, every sick or elderly member, feels this crisis as a personal tragedy, as if a tree had snapped at its main roots. No healthy community can possibly be built around a crumbling family structure.

9. Real tragedy can strike the partners if, utterly unprepared by previous experience, they suddenly collapse under this tremendous strain. Who is there to help mend the marriage if it breaks? One should not judge the partner who walks out, but one must admire that partner who stays on, battling for ways to provide for the children's daily life. The one-parent family is increasing at a terrifying rate and it is always only one step away from disaster.

10. If the mother has to go to hospital and there is no network of helpful neighbours to take in the children, no tribal structure in the background to safeguard the continuity of the child's life at home or at least in the neighbourhood, the 'Welfare' has to step in.

Uninvolved people have no vested interest in preventing their situation from deteriorating further; they withdraw into apathy via the path of minimum existence. Many thousands, young and old, live in this twilight state, prevented from ever fulfilling themselves because they are either (*a*) blocked, or (*b*) understimulated, or (*c*) impelled to opt out; some even suffer from all three conditions.

Such people may give no outward sign of being in a breakdown state, because they are fully law-abiding. In fact, such people are commonly thought of as good citizens. Yet any society which condemns many of its members to life-long immaturity and then uses the unhappy victims of its own failure (the unmarried mother, the one-parent family, delinquent youth, the mentally ill) as scapegoats, for others less unlucky to point their fingers at, is a society ethically sick. It will contaminate everyone who grows up in it. A culture of human warmth and solidarity must be substituted for our present culture of competition and withdrawal.

NEEDED: A NEW KIND OF GROUP
AND COMMUNITY WORK

What is needed in the renewed areas, as well as in new towns, is a new kind of community worker: a professional, trained to do a job of social reafforestation amongst the people living in the area, able to stimulate their latent leadership, to free their will to develop, and apply principles of group- and community-work in actual practice and as *they* see fit.

1. *Schools*: This implies a training for urban life which should have high priority in the educational system.

Our present school system ignores almost completely the social and the creative parts of human intelligence, focusing all its resources on the technical and abstract parts of intelligence. Modern man would find it difficult enough to survive without the use of technical and abstract intelligence; but without his social and creative intelligence he is utterly doomed to failure. The whole structure of community life is in danger of collapse if the socio-creative function is neglected, because it is this which enables the individual to get along with his fellow-beings and to discover new ways of self- and group-expression. It is this which turns houses into homes; today's houses are too often death-traps.

According to the Newsome Report, 50 per cent of children are being written off as failures because of the failure of the educational system. The proportion of such 'failures' among children is growing all the time. They are automatically excluded from opportunities which other children take for granted; and whole areas in which they live come to be regarded as failure areas, so reflecting failure on the people who live in these places. In this paper our special concern is for these 'failure' children: it is not that they are necessarily less educable than the 'successful' children of our present system, but that the social inadequacies imposed on them by their environment make them unable to compensate for it.

There is a major teaching job to be done for these children. They are mainly blocked off or understimulated, and thus they cannot develop socially. If we can help them to prove to themselves that they are potentially as able and gifted in their social and creative intelligence as others are in their technical and abstract intelligence, they will begin to find their satisfaction in participating constructively in the life of their community. The social climate which at present is so depressing could be made stimulating by the very people it has depressed so far, were they enabled emotionally and rationally to join in intelligent decision making. The precondition, however, is that they be made fully conscious of their environment and of their relationship to it. We call 'social education' the means we use to achieve this awareness within the schools. It is a training system starting at the beginning of secondary-school life, and covering a varied programme of observation, communication, activation, action-surveys, and finally group- and community-work, based on the young people's own concerns, inspired by their own sense of group responsibility and carried out by themselves. This they are more than able to do successfully when, after being taught a minimal amount of theory, they begin social surveys and social action, which in turn enhance their capacity to take in theoretical knowledge. Such theory enables people to evaluate their personal and social condition, and to take measures to improve it, should they decide that improvement is needed. No one can or should do this for them, as long as they can do it for themselves: taking out of their own hands the initiative to act must necessarily have a demoralizing effect. However much it may seem to be 'for their own good', any action decided on and carried out under someone else's direction merely increases the dependence of the one who receives on the one who gives.

2. *Adults*: When the principles of social education have to be imparted outside school, to adults, we refer to it as group and community training. Those who do the training are called 'community workers', or 'group workers', or 'liaison workers', according to whether they are working at the level of the extensive community, of the more immediate neighbourhood, or of the block. This new type of social helper or assistant performs a mainly catalytic function in an area, drawing into a common setting people who may have felt quite unrelated up to that point and who, although often acutely aware of their isolation, have been unable to do anything about it because they did not know how or where to begin.

Were these people to be manipulated into undertaking some kind of joint action which they had not had the chance to discuss and to decide on for themselves, the undermining of their dignity would cancel out any possible advantage resulting from the action. They would unconsciously be acting out Socrates' dictum: 'The unexamined life is not worth living.' If, however, they have a chance to be trained, advised, and helped to set up small pilot projects of their own as working models, they can from then on proceed under their own steam.

The shame-culture of today could be used in a positive sense: the ancient Greeks used shame as a weapon against the man who would not participate in the affairs of the community—they regarded him as an idiot. People today can be enabled to adopt a similar attitude to the social drone, however 'respectable' he may have been till now.

Group- and community-work helps people to go well beyond the ethically minimum concept of doing their minimum duty to gain their minimum rights. As responsible citizens they are able not only to invent new ways of helping themselves and others; they are also growing from a minimum to a maximum life (from existence to living) by applying their stimulated social and creative intelligence to the task of waking up their environment-dynamic. Potential abilities, previously dormant, create new structures and, within these, new avenues of expression; new ways of co-operation are invented and results obtained which no one would have thought remotely possible. Instead of feeling inadequate and therefore depressed as they were before, they are now able, in the words of a perceptive American, to see any social challenges before them as 'a series of great opportunities brilliantly disguised as insoluble problems'.

Training in group- and community-work is a means of sharing basic know-how in the field of community development, both with those who are experts and with those who actually live in a situation they want to change.

Experts and groups of socially-trained citizens can achieve real progress once they feel they are colleagues; once they begin to work together as real equals, for well-defined and constructive purposes, instead of straining against one another as rivals, seeking personal status at one another's expense.

COMMUNITY STRUCTURE AND PREVENTION OF SOCIAL BREAKDOWN

In the field of prevention of social breakdown, there is no large-scale planning today: there is a good deal of patching up, a good deal of smashing up, but in terms of prevention—nothing. Social action, whether preventive or constructive, can be successfully undertaken only if everyone whom it concerns is able to take part in the planning, the preparation and the actual carrying out of it. The function of the community workers is to *enable* this.

The community is structured on the one hand through its peer-groups and sub-cultures and on the other through its family groups, blocks, neighbourhoods, etc. Some people find their greatest security in the peer-group; that is, other people like themselves, who share their outlook, their interests and their needs; several peer-groups together (i.e. of teenagers, of mothers of pre-school children, of professionals, etc.) form sub-cultures which may extend far beyond national groupings and become international in character. To belong to a peer-group or to a sub-culture may be a life-saver for anyone who has special problems which others who have not experienced these problems cannot understand. For instance, the mother of an autistic child is more likely to entrust her child to the care of another mother who also has an autistic child than perhaps to her own mother.

Also, when there is no family group or affinity family

group (made up of people who, although not related, have chosen to live together as if they were), the peer-group can substitute its own protectiveness. For a secure family is the smallest and most basic form of community life. Within it, each member usually has different needs, according to age, temperament or condition, and can be linked to his own kind through membership in a peer-group of his choice. Yet the family life together, if it is a loving and understanding family, gives each member a sense of security through its shared experiences, shared memories and shared expectations for the future; it also gives mutual trust and patterns of responsibility, which express the members' sense of belonging to each other.

When the family group includes other families living in the same street, whose children play together, whose fathers are friends, whose mothers help each other out in all sorts of ways, the family unit grows into a neighbourhood group; several neighbourhood groups grow into a block; several blocks, into a community. Alternatively, a family may choose to link itself with another family in another part of the town or the area, for reasons of mutual interest or common concern: this link could be the beginning of another peer-group structure, and eventually, if the families decided to move in together or to emigrate together, they will lay the foundations of another community structure.

The fact is that every person and every family may take from and give to a variety of cultures at a variety of levels.

What matters is that the greatest possible number of people, at the base of the social pyramid, should be linked to one another, willing to act together responsibly, and able to communicate with people at other levels. Society then rests on a correspondingly broad and stable base. At the moment the opposite is true: the pyramid, precariously balanced on a narrow point made up of the experts and administrators who support it as best they can, is completely inverted; whilst the vast majority of people contribute little or nothing to their own common welfare or to the social health of their environment. The majority's apathy is as demoralizing to the professional 'givers' as to the 'Welfare' recipients. The result is a static or downright hostile relationship between experts and people.

The training we propose for families preparatory to rehousing is an exercise in preventive social education. Its purposes are: (a) to counteract the dangerous neurosis of self-centredness and dependence which does not permit them to feel or be aware of the needs of others (alienation); (b) to learn how, together with their peers and neighbours and friends, to assess common priorities in a changing environment; and (c) to understand constructive social action. Such training is a deliberate departure from the sterile objective of formal education, which can be reduced to (a) specialization and (b) conforming.

Society's real failure is summed up in that of the planners, who have failed to give proper consideration to the people's social needs. People are thrust into urban settings without any opportunity to become successfully urbanized; they are doomed to suffer sociosomatic illnesses (so often thought of as simply *psycho*somatic ailments), to break down as individuals and as groups, and to live out tragically and unnecessarily wasted lives.

SOME SUGGESTIONS FOR PRACTICAL APPLICATION

I. CRASH PROGRAMME OF SOCIAL EDUCATION

A crash programme of social education should be given

to people before they leave their old area. It should last for a week and have a follow-up after their arrival in the new area. If it is impossible to give this course before they move it should be given as soon as possible after their arrival. *The course's content* should include:

1. Sociodrama showing typical *distress situations* which can be played, preferably by youngsters from the old school, as part of their own preparation and also to help make parents and others who come aware of problems to be faced.

2. Public discussions of details unavoidably connected with rehousing; e.g. painting of new dwellings (how much of it could be done by the new tenants, if they desired), new furniture, the best use of room space; and *priorities* based on essentials first, necessities later and luxuries last.

3. *Legal and financial* aspects: the risks attached to hire purchase; sound budgeting, etc.

4. The *work* situation: what are the opportunities for men and women workers? Can new work be found? What arrangements exist for those who will need to go back to old work places if no new work is available?

5. *Transport* requirements and facilities connected with the work, shopping and leisure needs of each generation.

6. What facilities are needed to meet the *requirements of the children and young people*: (*a*) at home; (*b*) at school; (*c*) at play; (*d*) week-ends and holidays; (*e*) of latchkey children. What could be done to meet these: (*a*) by the parents; (*b*) by the youngsters; (*c*) by a mixed group of old and young.

7. *How to form groups and peer-groups*:
   a. at neighbourhood level;
   b. on a level of common *indignation*, of curiosity and doubt, for the purpose of improving certain conditions;
   c. mutual Uncle and Aunt schemes binding families

together which are not actually related except through their children and their own common need of security;

d. common workshops to build furniture;

e. common garages to repair vehicles;

f. common points system for exchange of equipment goods and services;

g. common attempts to keep neighbourhoods tidy;

h. common 'at homes'.

8. Using the scheme as a uniting factor to create the basis of a new community culture, *a survey could be organized* to find out:

a. How parents can help the school.

b. How the school can help the parents. Can youngsters help to run play-groups and supervise play-centres for children of pre-school age and all young children, especially during holidays?

c. What emergency arrangements exist for people who are suddenly taken ill.

d. What kind of service the young can give themselves.

e. What arrangements could be made for those especially interested in community leadership: e.g. morning 'adult' education for non-working mothers, and evening-school for other adults.

9. *Care*:

a. *by the elderly,* i.e. in terms of what the elderly can give to the community, to the young marrieds and to smaller children—as ersatz grandparents, etc.;

b. *for the elderly* in need of help or assistance. As the best defence against self-isolation and self-pity, other community services should only step in to do what the elderly may not be able to do for each other without hardship.

II. NEIGHBOURHOOD CENTRE

The Neighbourhood Centre might consist of a few rooms only, or a flat or a small house. It should serve approximately 3,000 people (the small village equivalent), roughly the area now served by an average primary school. It should serve many of the neighbourhood's day-by-day activities:

Morning: Small children's play-centre, or mothers' club. Lunch time: the elderly eat there and have their club.

Afternoon: Latchkey children play there and do their homework. Evenings: club meetings, adult courses.

It should run on a voluntary basis: volunteers, trained on group-work lines, can do this.

III. COMMUNITY CENTRE

1. A Community Centre catering for a whole community (i.e. four to ten neighbourhoods according to the size of the Centre) could be run by a part-time worker and week-end volunteer workers who were members of the community itself. The Community Centre would give rise to the development of special-interest (peer-) groups which would make life more intensive and interesting all round; e.g. women's groups; political, religious, artistic groups; groups for fun, relaxation and interest, all potentially contributing to new sub-cultures in the making. The catalytic function of the clergy should be in evidence at this community level.

2. The Community Centre can help to channel the broad streams of thought and activity into events of interest to the greatest number of people, but much of the 'capillary' work will be done through the Neighbourhood Centres which will be nearer to the people's daily lives. Eventually it should be possible to gauge the improvement in the

essential quality of community life achieved, by the pride of the people in 'our community'.

3. Those who cannot participate in a normal life—the socially handicapped or inadequate of any age, including sub-normals, 'delinquents', alcoholics, minority members who are potential scapegoats, or isolates—can be helped to survive by the community's neighbourly and deliberate helpfulness. Social tolerance and conscious solidarity in action are the best ways to teach the young to become responsible and mature adults.

4. As part of a deliberate policy, is the community willing to accept full responsibility for anybody within its neighbourhoods who is in difficulty or in potential danger? The proof of true communal culture lies in the community's readiness to look after *anyone* in need.

5. Would the community be willing, as part of its outward purpose, to apply itself in some way to helping a group of people far away, to participate in the actual affairs of another community, hospital or orphanage far removed, which needs more than monetary help, and show its interest in practical ways, e.g. 'twinning', corresponding, visiting, etc.?

6. Can a real Centre be produced, in which a developing community can look forward to at least one major interesting activity every evening, and other minor ones suiting different tastes (but not only bingo-type)? These might include:

   a. a public report to the community by its leaders every six to eight weeks, or more often if the need is felt;

   b. concerts, by outsiders or community members—e.g. choir, folk song and dancing, chamber music, ballet, opera;

   c. theatre and sociodrama evenings;

   d. sports evenings.

After a short period every interested person should be

involved and feel that he is genuinely a growing and contributing part of a growing whole.

7. Help freely given and freely received by all, as necessary, is what makes a community life rich, interesting and stimulating to its members. They should experience in their community life not only security and joy but also stimulating opportunities to develop a sense of responsibility and to grow in personality. For this purpose social education in group and community work provides a common 'language' of informed understanding and an appreciation on the part of everyone of the dangers involved in letting a few people take over. Commercial organizations are only able to exploit the community's wish for some joy in life because there are usually too few alternatives available.

CONCLUSION

The wholistic view is a strikingly clear one once it is denuded of the confusing detail which clouds the specialist's view. There must be trained an army of generalists; namely, people skilled in the understanding of the cohesive factors of society, people able to generate human warmth and social sanity.

Just as the judge is at liberty to accept or to reject the advice of experts given in court, and the jury is at liberty to accept or reject this advice and also the judge's summing-up, so we, the community, composed of individuals and groups, professional and unprofessional, should be at liberty to accept or to reject new specialist methods, diagnoses and cures as we see fit. This is more than our right: it is our responsibility not to leave the running of the country, any more than the running of our personal lives, to our 'betters'. These 'betters', who often live a life far removed from others in rarefied, mandarin-type seclusion, have induced a sense of inferiority in ordinary people, and made them feel that they are not worthy to participate in the making of decisions which may affect their own ultimate survival, social health and the development of their children and of their loved ones.

This is what we call the second Welfare State. The professional equipment of the first Welfare State should be preserved, but now the life-patterns of people need to be worked out anew *by the people themselves.*

Democracy exists for 'urbanized' nations, only when we can all be partners and colleagues in urban living, each person and each group equally important for the whole. This does not come naturally in our present pattern, which goes in the opposite direction, but must depend on training, common planning and common action, by the people and for the people.

5. The People of God and The Cities of Man

BY

RAYMOND PANIKKAR

Professor of World Religions, Harvard University

'*But the hour will come—in fact is here already—when true worshippers will worship the Father in spirit and truth: that is the kind of worshipper the Father wants.*'
JOHN 4:23

HOW *people* and *cities* relate to one another is the theme of this conference. The shortest way between two points is the straight line, but the straight line always passes through the stars, because our universe is curved. Thus the ultimate problem of our conference is the relation between Man and God. The title of my contribution itself expresses the risk of attempting a real theology of urbanism: 'The People of God and the Cities of Man'. How can man live in the city so as to fulfil his being a person? This is the same problem stated in other words.

After stating—

The Problem in three particular aspects:
  1. The role of the church in the modern city.
  2. The tower of Babel.
  3. The *Metanoia*, Conversion.

I shall attempt to describe—

The People of God according to its two fundamental categories:
1. Space.
2. Time.

and finally—

The Cities of Man in their threefold function:
1. Communication.
2. Communion.
3. Transcendence.

THE PROBLEM

'When he came in sight of the city, he wept over it'
LUKE 19:41

1. 'THE ROLE OF THE CHURCH
IN THE MODERN CITY'

With these words Canon Stephen Verney, the Director of Studies of this conference, summed up the ultimate purpose of our meeting. I would like to essay a straightforward answer to this question. But to be concrete and specific I shall try to tackle the question from the humblest and most realistic point of view. The *church* of my discourse is going to be *primarily* not the Kingdom of God, the Spouse of Christ, the People of God, but simply what the people, to the amazement or scandal of theologians, still go on calling the *church*, i.e. that material place, that stone or wooden building, which I could equally call the *altar*.

I understand by altar not only the place for the Sacrifice, but also the place for the Preacher, the Book, the Idol and the like. In fact, when I say church, I mean church, temple, cathedral, mosque, synagogue, tabernacle, joss-house, pagoda, chapel, shrine, palace, pyramid, stupa, dagoba, house of prayer, etc. In short: holy place.

By doing this I am not only eliminating the danger of generalization, but I am hoping to speak about the function of the church in the modern city in a way which makes sense to everybody: the role of a special place in the city for a purpose which, being differently formulated, transcends all merely pragmatic functions and strives to help man to become more fully what he is meant to be.

Our question amounts to asking what is the concrete role of a sacred structure in the life of the city. Does it need to be, first of all, a material structure? Is not religion a private matter, a question of the heart? Have we not, East and West, North and South, suffered enough from those types of religiosity which tie religion down with the political and temporal structures? Can man still be considered a sacred animal? Are we not outgrowing the age of religion?

I shall not argue now that it all depends on what idea we have of religion, the sacred and the like. I shall simply attempt to show some basic points which could be developed into a foundation for a theology of the city.

2. THE TOWER OF BABEL

In the fourth chapter of Genesis we have some interesting suggestions. All of them lead us to think that the Bible and Christianity at large have a proclivity towards agriculture, nature and rural culture, as against technique, cities and urban civilization.

The city begins to be the city of man against God. 'Abel was a shepherd, Cain a tiller of the ground' (Gen. 4: 2). The former was blessed, the latter did not find sympathy with God. This same God's animosity against the city dwellers is visible in the later passage of Sodom and Gomorrah (Gen. 19).

Cain has slain his brother. After the death of the other,

he is afraid. He fears everything; the earth, animals, other people. But a man does not live alone in this world. Cain, and with him man, now feels he has to protect himself. The text goes on: 'Cain knew his wife, and she conceived and bore Enoch; and *he built a city*, and called the name of the city after his son Enoch' (Gen. 4:17). To build a city is to give birth. Both the biological and the cultural act are sacred acts, are in a certain sense a blasphemy, a challenge to the Creator and at the same time a re-enactment of the primordial act. Both need propitiation. The mother has to be 'cleansed', the city-founder has to perform a rite, a sacrifice, etc. The history of religions teaches us of the cosmic and religious significance of the building of a city.

Man after his exile from paradise is a rival of God and the city is his fortress. Cities are not only the places of vice, corruption and power; they are also the substitutes for the city of God, luring men and allowing them to forget that 'here we have no lasting city, but we seek the city which is to come' (Heb. 13:14).

The episode of the tower of Babel (Gen. 11:1–9) expresses this in the most forceful way. The tower of Babel is the beginning of the socializing of man. The building of the city is discontinued because it is being done under the presupposition of reaching heaven, i.e. of escaping the human condition and isolating man from his neighbour. It is an escalation into heaven and not a descent of the divine. Man wants to become God, without waiting for God to become a man.

Before Babel words were a kind of private property. The 'words were few' says the Bible. They were the possession of a private group. Communication was the exchange of goods and of words which had, as it were, private value. Only the confusion of tongues made words the common property of everybody and destroyed the individual or

closed-groups ownership of them. A city made of individual houses or isolated streets is not a human city; a
tower climbing up to heaven is not a city; a word which is
only mine, or which only my clan understands, is not a
word—it has great value as a precious thing, but is not a
word. A word has value if it is not mine, and others can
use and have it.

No wonder that Christians have all too often been
absent from the building of the earthly cities. To build a
city on earth would have been considered as a sin in the
early Christian centuries: *'In terra degunt, sed in caelo
civitatem suam habent'* says the Epistle to Diognetes
(V, 9). Or again: *'civitas in terra peregrina, in caelo
fundata'*, would add St Augustine (Serm. 105, No. 9).[1]

Only by Pentecost is Babel overcome (John 11:52;
Acts 2:1–9). Only by descent of the divine city and not by
an escape from the human condition, only by understanding one another and not by speaking the same
language can the tension become creative (Rev. 7:9;
etc.). True religiousness is a constant fight against the
divine, as was the case with Moses, Abraham, Jacob, Paul,
etc., to extort from him, as it were, what they were seeking.

A new spirituality is required in our times: not that of
building a city of man to match the city of God, nor of
climbing up to heaven, but of getting really incarnated
into flesh, into matter, into a city which is also the like-
ness, image and being of the divine.

3. THE METANOIA, CONVERSION

The present-day situation is one of *qualitative transformation*. There is a mutation taking place before our
eyes on almost all levels of existence. I have to limit myself
to our concrete problem. A modern city is not just a large

[1] For this and many other citations, as well as the theological implications, see my book *Patriotismo y Cristiandad*, Madrid (Rialp) 1961.

village. There is a certain quantitative growth which brings about a qualitative mutation. Our problem today is not just one of adjusting man to the 'second-degree' machine as we were formerly accustomed to the simple 'first-degree' tool. It is no longer a mere question of adaptation or correction. Nor is it a question of simply moralizing the issues, and saying that man has to live a 'human' life in a city of five million or to utilize automation and the splitting of the atom for good purposes.

To walk at 5 miles per hour or to drive at 50 miles per hour may still be on the same scale, but the problem becomes qualitatively different if we travel at 500 or 5,000 miles per hour. With these latter speeds man can now do things which he simply could not have done before even if he had lived on earth for 300 years. Ninety per cent of mankind only 100 years ago lived their whole life within 50 miles of their birth places, a fact which had not only sociological but also anthropological consequences.

The growth of a city today cannot proceed any longer by juxtaposition as it has generally until now. The building of a city today, or its mutation from a traditional to a modern city, is again a sacred and ritual act: it is a new creation, a real foundation of something not pre-existent. In a word, cities are changing and are changing radically. So the church in the city has also to change, and to change thoroughly. If the city is a community where people live together, this same description applies to the church. Between church and city the relation is an intimate one.

Thus it is not enough to change the style of the church or the orientation of the altar or the deployment of the clergy. Not only the 'rubrics' have to be changed but also the 'nigrics', not only the procedure and the protocol, but also the shape and the content.

The *metanoia*, the conversion I am advocating, could

perhaps be translated rather by *revolution*, by a radical change in orientation and by upsetting previously accepted patterns. This *metanoia* has to transform the very sense of the sacred, as well as the sense of matter and the meaning of 'church' and 'religion'.

The sacred is not to be any longer the 'segregated' portion versus the profane, the *pro-fanum*; this opposition has to be transformed into a creative tension within every being and inside any situation. The sacred has to cease to be sacred if by that we mean not secular, and the profane has to dispense with being opposite the *fanum*, the temple, the sacred. From a mythical starting point in which everything was sacred we have to revert to a moment in which all is secular, thus overcoming the dichotomy without blurring the creative tension.

Similarly matter is no longer to be seen as the opposite and enemy of the spirit or as the expression of imperfection or even as evil, but rather as the very body of the spirit, as its expression and playing ground. The human spirit expresses itself in its body as does the divine spirit in its world. The intellectual separation between matter and spirit cannot be allowed to crystallize into a metaphysical duality.

The church must also be seen neither as mainly an organization, nor as exclusively an invisible and purely spiritual entity. It is a living organism with a body, having members of many different kinds.

In order to avoid misunderstandings let me say from the outset that I would like to understand 'church' always as a predicate and not as a subject. Or, in other words, when I say for instance that the church is the meeting place between men, or the place for celebration, what I am saying is that whenever a real meeting takes place, wherever an authentic festival is celebrated, there is church, that is church. The *metanoia* works at the renewal of every traditional proposition concerning the church. The church is indeed the place of salvation, because any place where salvation takes place is church.

Nor is religion merely a special field of human activity, a set of rituals of whatever kind—but it is that kernel existing in every being, and giving *real* value to any authentically human act.

We may now focus this discussion of the problem upon our concrete issue: if modern urbanism has as its role to free man from his many constraints, then the church has a function to perform in this very process of liberation.

THE PEOPLE OF GOD

'For us, our homeland is in heaven, and from heaven comes the saviour we are waiting for, the Lord Jesus Christ.'

PHILIPPIANS 3:20

The need for a radical change should not be ignored on the excuse that the optimal conditions for a change are not present. There is a danger in elaborating an ideal system, and imagining the role of a perfect church. The church has to act at all levels and under all conditions. Cathedrals may still be useful for a long time, and catacombs may also be needed. The house-altar may still perform a meaningful function, and the dining-room may perhaps be the most suitable place for the eucharistic celebration. No monolithic or ideal solution is going to give us the real answer. It is not a question of proposing ready-made recipes or of giving technical advice, for this is a matter in which organic growth and the common working out of living experience, rather than of preconceived ideas, is essential.

A city has to fulfil several functions: it has to be a place for dwelling, growing (education), transportation (and movement), recreation (and play), existing and exchanging spiritual and material goods—a place where man as person can live in community. The city is the *natural* place where modern man lives. Up to recent times, the city was rather the artificial and exceptional place for man's life, the majority of mankind living in villages. Today almost the opposite is the case. The city is the earthly place transformed for human life in our times; it is, in one word, the place of civilization. The culture or cultivation of the soil, or of the soil of man, becomes civil life, civic virtues, civilization.

Now human life has not only individual and spiritual value, it has also social and material values. The city embodies all these values, and the church is the servant in the city, providing the atmosphere, creating the climate, and offering the place where these values can grow and develop harmoniously.

From this point of view the role of the church is a double one. On the one hand it has to provide for a harmonious development of the different human dimensions. It has to counterbalance and complement the different activities of human life. When society at large, for instance, neglected education and physical welfare, the churches were schools and hospitals for those in need. Now that these functions are taken over by government or by society at large, the church should no longer consider this field as its specific one and could concentrate, for instance, on providing a place for friendship, disinterested human relations, love and the like. On the other hand it may be said that there is still a peculiar religious dimension, a sense of verticality, which may be cultivated in and by the church. Because God, religion and the churches have been too often bulwarks of conservatism, or because our picture of God has been a sort of *Deus ex machina* who provides ready answers to human fallibility, we cannot be too careful in describing this vertical dimension or this openness to transcendence; but one abuse would not justify another.

The basis for the following reflections will be an anthropological conception of man, which I could summarize by saying that man is not an individual, not a substance, but a person, i.e. a centre of relations with others, with the world and yet non-finite, ever open. Among these relationships two are now going to guide our discussion: *space* and *time*, not as external conditions but as constitutive dimensions of man.

The city planner is a human engineer who deals with material no less human than does the medical doctor healing a human person. The church in the city is that material structure in which the human person complements, counterbalances and deepens his humanity. It belongs to the mystery of Incarnation that the full human life has not only a spiritual or intellectual side, but also a spatio-temporal co-ordinate.

I. THE SACRED SPACE

'In the spirit, he took me to the top of an enormous high mountain, and showed me Jerusalem, the holy city, coming down from God out of heaven.'

REVELATION 21:10

Man is a spatial being. He does not only live in space; his life is also spatial, expresses itself spatially, and needs space. Man has been aliented from space. A new relationship with space has been developed. Nowadays man is losing his fear of space and getting nearer to it by dominating it. Space is no longer a barrier outside but a limit within. The sacred space is no longer the consecrated space reserved for special purposes. The sacred space is the human space, the real space which man consecrates by filling it.

There must be in man space for privacy as well as space for celebration, transactions and communications. There is something which could be called a social space and something a private space, and if traditionally it was the social, it is today the private which is becoming more and more the sacred and religious space. Once upon a time practically all social and public buildings were religious buildings. The king or ruler was a sacred person precisely because he was a public person. Now it seems that almost the opposite is the case: the private space seems to be more sacred than the public one and this latter, the *res publica*, seems to be fully de-sacralized.

The function of the church is to provide such private and public sacred spaces, human spaces. The church of the modern city may well be, on the one hand, the 'basilica', the cathedral, the big building, the stadium. On the other hand it may also be the quiet room of a house, the inner chamber of a compound, the common room of a basement, the small chapel of a complex building.

What modern urbanism has called the 'core', the core of a city (which the Italians have simply rendered by '*cuore*'), is really the church and might be called again 'church', not because the clerical element is present there, but because by definition the heart of a city cannot but be its religious centre: its soul.

When I say that the church provides the meeting place of the human in man, when I affirm that the soul of the city is the church, I am not saying that the existing church or the present-day chapel (or whatever) is that heart, but exactly the converse: wherever this meeting takes place, wherever man overcomes his ego-centredness and is open, sideways and upwards, there is church.

The heart of the city cannot be mainly the commercial centre, or the financial district, or the confessional chapel. It has to be a space for life; open, universal, human; incarnating concrete but universal values, and with a certain priority to the festive and joyous aspect of man. It has to be a place for contemplation and celebration. The common, the plaza, the central square where the elders can discuss, the old contemplate, the women murmur, the young love and the children play, where justice can be done, men meet, people pray and celebrate, where people can, in one word, live, this is the core, this is the church, this is that vital centre the architect is looking for and the city planner looking after.

I would like to point out two features of this space:

a. *Limited.* There is no space without limits. The limits, and even the human limitations, make the space. We should be losing sight of human nature and destroying man if we were to forget his concreteness and his fidelity to the soil.

The church in the city has to be a limited space, a concrete place. It cannot be just a spirit, a climate, a feeling. It is limited by walls, lights, sound (or the absence of it), a special location, a peculiar place. The church must not pretend to be everywhere.

'Limited' means also discreet, humble, small. The time for majestic temples is, by and large, over. The existing ones may still perform a certain function, and the cities which have conserved them have probably preserved also the tradition which renders them meaningful, but for the modern city they are neither important nor urgent priorities.

The church in the modern city wants to be, first of all, a small place for recollection, and for prayer in private and public, where a person can go to regain his soul and a group may gather to sing and celebrate and speak or simply be. It needs to be a living symbol for the sacred, for this deepest and ever-transcending dimension of man. The church is not only a place to visit or to see; it is also a place to sit in and be in. A shrine, a monument in a square, a corner in a green area, a small temple, a commemorative place, a fountain, a garden, a wall, a building, a basement or a top floor, a window in a shopping centre, an office in a great compound—all this can be the church, and fulfil the function I am describing.

To conclude, the limitation of space stands for *interiorization* and inwardness. This space should lead not to introversion, but to intimacy and to the discovery of the inner depth of one's self.

Modern man needs to learn again to be *alone*, precisely in order to be able to overcome isolation; he needs to enter into real solitude, and only there will he learn not to hate himself and to reach communication—the first condition of which is to have something to communicate.

b. Open. One of the greatest dangers of the church, at all levels, is that of being a closed society, a sect, another pressure-group. The church of the modern city has to symbolize universality by a spatial openness. It cannot be a private property, nor a closed compound in an enclosure of walls, virtue, money, culture, initiation, or a coterie of believers. In fact, the limitation of space must not contradict its openness. The operative word today is pluralism—a healthy pluralism which does not disrupt harmony and unity. To realize the universal in the particular, or to discover the particularities in the universal, is a phenomenon of authenticity and of wisdom.

The church which I am trying to describe is a place of recreation, as more than one Christian generation has felt, or a 'festival hall' as it was called at the beginning of the spread of Christianity, when Pachomios's monks wanted to build a church in the village of their community.

A word to Christians may be in place here; the open church I am proposing is not syncretistic or reduced to a minimalistic religiosity in order not to hurt anybody's feelings. It implies first of all catholicity, universality; a transparence of means and aims; and an interpretation of the message of Christ which is all-inclusive rather than nearly all-exclusive. It means, secondly, real service, which precludes dictating how the other ought to be ministered upon; it means serving him and his needs as they appear to him. The mission of the Christian is to serve mankind and this means to help a Hindu to be a better Hindu, a so-called Humanist a better Humanist, and indeed a fellow-Christian a better Christian. Present-day Christian ecumenism is the first step towards a genuinely ecumenical ecumenism.

How to give urbanistic expression to all this is, in my opinion, one of the most important tasks of our times.

A whole conception of the liturgy is implied here. I will mention only one single aspect, which I would call communion, over against the excommunication and the *disciplina arcani* of the ancient times.

A peculiar aspect of almost all ancient liturgies, and of practically all religions, was that of excommunication, i.e. of keeping aside, when not actually throwing outside, those who for one reason or another did not belong to the special rite. The door of the church had to be closed before the beginning of the mysteries, and the catechumens were not allowed to remain inside. Faith, belonging to a particular church, permission to enter a particular temple —all were privileges, rights of the few. The superiority and sublimity of a church were symbolized by the thickness of its gates and the difficulty of its entrance.

The church of the modern city has to reckon with a totally different concept: the space is not there to separate but to unite; the altar, the presbytery and the pulpit are not to be segregated, or maintained at a certain distance and in a reverential twilight. The liturgy of the church in the contemporary city is not one of segregation, hierarchy and excommunication, but of communion.

2. THE SACRED TIME

'Jesus answered, "The right time for me has not come yet, but any time is the right time for you".'   JOHN 7:6

Man is not only a spatial creature, he is also a temporal being. This is the stuff out of which he is made—for the time being.

One of the characteristics of modern man is mobility and speed. He changes his habitat, his place, his habits; he travels, he actually flies. The rhythmic pattern of agricultural man—the seasons, the moon and even the sun—are hardly of any relevance to modern Western man. The city dweller follows—for good or for ill—his own rhythm, adapted from the pulsation of the machine rather than from the beats of the cosmos. The modern city is not only a place to dwell; it is also an occasion to move and to move on.

The church of our cities has to be both an expression of this new rhythm and a counterbalance to it. It cannot paralyse the tempo of man, but neither can it allow human time to be dehumanized and lose its specificity. Most of the churches are incapable of keeping up with the times, because they cannot put up with modern human time. Time has been allowed to freeze and to be spatialized, to be sometimes also 'spiritualized' and thus die.

I am not advocating ambulant churches in trucks and mobile loudspeakers. I mean, first of all, the experience of time as a human reality, and as an integral part of the person.

It is not simply by reducing his tempo that man is going to come to himself; nor is it by curtailing his speed

that the church is going to achieve anything, but by helping man to discover his own rhythm and enter into synchrony with reality, be it human, mechanical or cosmic.

First of all, man could easily regain the experience of the
heterogeneity of time, the personal conviction that from
5 to 6 is not the same as from 11 to 12; that not all
times are equal precisely because persons are different,
and that to know the signs of the time amounts to know-
ing reality.

Secondly, that time is itself, and not space, precisely
because it cannot be overseen, circumwalled, embraced.
It is not for us to know the time (Acts 1 : 7). We have to
live time, to consume it, to kill it, in order to survive.

Sacred time was until recently a *social time*, a time for
celebration. It is now *free time*—and personal time is the
only possible one for the festival. The festival cannot be
forced nor imposed upon us; it has to be the spontaneous
explosion of an inner urge, the free manifestation of an
inward joy. Free time is not just there because one has not
got to work. Free time is really freeing; it is free because it
liberates from the constraints of inhuman factors.

How to express the temporal aspect of the church in
the modern city is a difficult problem indeed. I may however suggest a few lines of development, or rather a few
moments of growth.

The first observation concerns the sovereignty of the
church over time, or again in a more concrete way, the
possibility of overseeing the true dimensions of time and
thus mastering it.

What I am saying is this: the church represents the
revolutionary moment in society and in the city. Precisely
because the church claims to incarnate a trans-temporal
value it makes room for change and should not be afraid
of it.

I have spoken before of *metanoia,* the translation of

which could well be *revolution*, if this latter word had not already been exploited.

The church has to be the symbol of change, and for speedy change when the situation requires it, because passive resignation to a violent situation, or mere complacence with an unjust *status quo*, can be more unjust and violent than the positive effort to change it. Let us not forget that pulling out an arrow may be more painful than shooting it.

The transcendence that the church claims to incarnate allows it to overcome entanglements, to break attachments, and to channel contingent situations towards more desirable conditions. And in fact most of the revolutionary movements in Christianity as elsewhere are connected with churches, in spite of the fact that when the church becomes an instrument of power, the people handling it may easily become conservatives.

Modern urbanology begins to discover that cities like men are also mortal, and that buildings like human beings have a limited life-span. The church should be there to stress a certain consciousness of provisionality, and a dynamic of growth. I am not advocating, obviously, permanent scaffolding on unfinished projects. I am pleading for a whole spirituality of *exodus*, for a mood of pilgrimage, a certain nomadic factor indispensable for the growth and development of human life.

This mood I am speaking of could be described as a style of life which reckons with death as a normal factor, without being afraid of it or artificially hiding its reality. It is a style which does not despise life, which does not dispense with the effort of building up a better world on all scales, but which considers that the value and the beauty of human life and of all human constructions lie precisely in the fact of their transitoriness, dynamism, growth and change. It is a style of life which does not hunt after the eternal on earth. Ideas are not everlasting, nor are stones or cities perennial. The time dimension should always be remembered, not only as something to go through, but as a factor which itself goes through all created structures.

In other more 'urbanological' terms it could be said that one of the functions of the church is to be a real symbol for the transitoriness of the city itself, and of all its structures which have to be reformed and renewed from time to time. *Ecclesia semper est reformanda*, meaning that the city also *semper est perficienda*. Or, in more concrete words, the town planners should not build too permanently; they should provide for necessary restructurings in order to meet the needs of living people.

In a word, the city of man has to be authentically a city of men and for men—not for angels, nor a substitute for the city of God.

The Festival. Time is a human dimension, wisdom is to detect the true rhythm of things, and joy is to move—to dance—according to that rhythm. If there were only one civic function which the church should—or could—undertake in our day, I would say that this is not education, or welfare or charities, but the inspiration and arrangement of the human celebration, of the civic festival. The feast—the holy day, the joy, the anti-economic, anti-individualistic and anti-utilitarian activity *par excellence* —is one of the most fundamental human and religious categories, of which the church should be a living symbol.

We are seriously concerned with working towards a better world, and rightly so; but we should remember that even more important than to construct the world is to live in it, to enjoy it, to live the world, and to experience that man and the universe are so marvellously 'made' that even if our situation is far from being optimal or just, it is still a gift, a blessing, a rapture and a joy simply to live, to be here, to assist at this birth, to exist in this hour, and to share in this divine venture.

The church is not only the place for celebration, it is also the time for the festival. And again here, as with the problem of change and revolution, the church is or should be precisely equipped to perform this function, for a double reason.

First, because celebration can be sincerely enjoyed only where there is a certain unconcern with immediate things and burning problems. Only where a sense of proportion does not allow us to be overwhelmed by day-to-day problems, can the human heart rejoice and celebrate. But this perspective can only be acquired if in man there is room for something other than his immediate cares. The church symbolizing this ever-unfinished aspect of man provides the ground which makes celebration possible—avoiding the dangers of the would-be festival (the orgy) which tries to stifle the cares of human existence. Celebration is neither a narcotic for our sufferings nor an outlet for our instincts; it is rather an expression of our internal and deepest nature.

Second, and still more important, the church is the time of celebration, because any authentic festival is the synthesis of three times. There is no celebration without a certain commemoration—*of the past*—which is re-enacted—*in the present*—in view of a hope *for the future* restructuring our lives. All these three times, like the mythological three worlds, are included in any celebration. Faith, Hope and Love are its basic elements. Without them there is no feast possible.

The function of the church seems to me to be fundamentally that of providing all the possible conditions for the human celebration. Man has to transcend his empirical and ego-ridden self if he is going to be able to celebrate. It is here that the function of the liturgy becomes of truly human proportions.

With very few exceptions there are hardly any meaningful civic liturgies today, or if we prefer, liturgies which are both a work and a play, a celebration and an event for the inhabitants of our cities. We go on following past traditions, fortunately still alive and reviving in some places, and we scarcely have the imagination to move beyond rural and agricultural patterns which have played such an important role in the past. The human person cannot live without rites and liturgy—and the older forms are, to say the least, insufficient. A fascinating task for the church is open here.

Needless to say, when I speak of liturgy and rite I do not mean protocol and ritualism, much less mere 'etiquette' of bygone ages. Nor am I suggesting a new committee for liturgy. I am pleading for real liturgy, which is life and celebration. The preparation of such liturgy would rather consist in removing obstacles and providing favourable conditions than in building platforms or scoring a certain type of music. The spirit blows where it wills and we may not know its direction. Of one thing however we can be sure, that it blows.

The Journey. Do not misunderstand me. I am not saying that the function of the church is to be an amusement agency. The church is neither the nurse nor the clown of mankind—though it may be a bit of both. What I want to emphasize is that the feast is a religious category *par excellence*; and the very fact that, in the West at least, people hide themselves from the established religions when they amuse and enjoy themselves is a very bad sign indeed for the vitality and relevance of such religions.

Whatever the reason for this may be, I wish to complete the previous point by stressing that time is not an external human category, but the very stuff out of which man is made, for the *time being*. It would be a lopsided view to consider man *only* as an historical being, but it would be equally onesided to hold that his temporality is something extrinsic to man.

As with space, so with time—it has also to be interiorized or rather assimilated so that man can grow. Maturity is not reached by just skating on time but by eating it up, by assimilating it. It is the sacrifice of time that enables man to overcome time, moment after moment, day by day.

It is not enough to celebrate the holidays in a proper manner; every day has to be a holy journey, and every moment a temporal opening towards the fullness of time.

The role of the church in the modern city has very much to do with the constant journeying of the citizen, in his movements of work and of relaxation, of joy as well as of suffering, in his times of solitude as well as of company and fellowship.

The altar of every church, the altar which the first Christians boasted they did not need to construct out of stone because their bodies were the proper temples of the Holy Spirit, the altar in whatever form and shape, has an inward relation with the human heart—which is incidentally the most mobile of man's organs.

What modern architects and urbanologists call the *human scale* could here be rendered as the *human rhythm*. The church has to offer that moment when our hearts may be tuned up again to their surroundings: men, nature and machinery. The church has to offer the possibility of a *synchrony*—a foundation for personal serenity and collective peace—with the world around us. Its function here might be considered as threefold, to 'attune'—to 'atone'—man with the biological, the mechanical and cosmic rhythm. Man has this stupendous capacity of being able to live in a polymorphic world, and it is for the church to hold the harmony. The human journey on earth is *idiorhythmic*. The church has here the mission of a mediator, for it is the mediator between those three rhythms. Church is that 'place' where rural man is 'speeded up' in order that he may be able to 'catch up' and not perish in the modern world. Church is—again—that 'place' where urban man is 'cooled down' in order that he may not explode and split his personality in schizophrenic fancies. Church is—still further—that 'place' where the journey is tuned up to the cosmic wheels so that disharmony may not prevail.

In other words, church is that peculiar laboratory where man loses his fear of himself, of the machine and of the universe. According to circumstances this may take the form of a city council integrating a ghetto into the life of the whole civic population, or of a university reintegrating the 'cultured' generation into a new relationship with nature and rescuing them from the ghetto of scholarship, or of a trade union struggling for the *ontonomy* [sic!] of the human rhythm over against the demands of the machine and productivity, or indeed of a traditionally sacred place offering reintegration and self-awareness.

Am I saying that the function of the church is that of a public relations office? I am rather suggesting that the public relations office is an ecclesiastical activity of the church in the modern city. Is not the church meeting-place, mediatorship? There is today a particular stewardship for which provision has to be made in the modern city, and all these agencies are performing that particular role of the church.

To sum up: to redeem time is an old Pauline injunction. The city planner has also got his ecclesiastical task, that of providing room for the human *idiorhythm* in the megalopolis of our times.

As for how—that, I think, is the reason for which we met here . . .

THE CITIES OF MAN

'I saw the holy city, and the new Jerusalem, coming down from God out of heaven, as beautiful as a bride all dressed for her husband.'   REVELATION 21 :2

The city of God was once upon a time the goal of man. It was so much so, that even those who did not believe in it wanted to build on earth precisely that very city of God —entering thus into competition and conflict with the believers in the city of God. Once upon a time—and here the clocks of history are not all set by Greenwich—the church stood for that city of God in heaven, in the skies, in the future or in the hearts.

The tremendous transformation going on before our eyes is that the church does not want to be that eschatological sign only, or even mainly, but it claims to be so seriously at the service of man, that it is ready to forgo all talk about the city of God if men do not believe any longer in the celestial Jerusalem. Indeed the church will say that the ultimate meaning of the city of God amounts to the same as what now goes under other names.

Whatever this may be, the modern city of man does not want to be an imitation on earth of the city of God; it wants to be a fully human city, and it has given up the ideal of escalating to heaven. The new ideal is a secular one, not in competition with the sacred but replacing it— restoring thus the original myth in which there was no distinction between the sacred and the profane. All was sacred. Now all is secular. Ultimately it comes to the same. The sacredness today is concentrated upon man. Man is the sacred being—in the final analysis because Man is more than man. Traditional Christians would call it the theandric mystery.

Cutting very short a long story, I would say that we are entering now into a new era as regards this relationship between the city of God and the city of Man.

Curiously enough St Augustine in spite of his dualism of the two cities, begins his monumental work by saying that the city of God 'lives by faith in this fleeting age of ours'. It is by faith in fact that the God of Israel promises to marry his people (Hosea 2 : 16), and the symbol of a city being the spouse of God is a common symbol in the history of religion. Without going outside Christianity one finds the Book of Revelation full of this symbolism (cf., 17:5; 17:18; 21:10, etc.).

The time of the espousals has come, so that both may now become one flesh. The central incarnational event of Christian faith can be rendered by saying not only that the Logos became flesh, but also that he became city: the city of men, at least since he 'planted his tent among us', can well be considered as the city of God.

We have to interrupt our exploration of this vein in order to come back to a concrete theology of urbanism.

The idea behind what follows is this: not only theology but also urbanism is at the service of man, and the principles for a theology of urbanism will have to be derived from a theological anthropology. The foundation of what follows could be summed up by saying that the human being is a personal being and thus a centre of relationships, a crossroads of relatedness and not an individual, a substance.

As for our concrete theme, I would distinguish three moments of importance for the role of the church in the city.

I. COMMUNICATION—TECHNOPOLIS

Man needs communication, exchange, commerce in order to live a meaningful and authentic human life. This communication is required at all levels.

I am being only realistic if I say that the driving force in the development of our modern cities is the growth and fostering of such communication. The city becomes a *technopolis* in order to make possible those exchanges of goods, persons, ideas, etc. Mass media, transport media, education procedures and the like, are all communication devices for news, persons, ideas, goods. Industry and commerce, including of course finance, are intrinsically related to communication.

Now, we know that all these techniques sometimes blur the deeper and more personal exchanges. The mission of the church is to help to channel the flow of communication so that it shall never reach saturation point (as in some affluent societies people begin to think it has already done), not to stifle those other exchanges which being more (or at least equally) important are more subtle or fragile or delicate to 'transport'.

In other words the role of the church is not that of putting barriers to the flow of information, but that of collaborating for the transformation of *information into communication*. Without a certain preparation, information can be simply a foreign body invading our organism without any message.

This involves a complex function of co-ordinating human needs, of providing a structure for a harmonious development of such needs, and of offering the right context in which the aforesaid transformation from information into communication can take place. A certain scale of values and a list of priorities seem here unavoidable.

This seems to me a basic function of the church: not that of imposing a preconceived set of values, but that of offering a market-place where these values could be discussed, forged and decided upon. The church should be able to provide such a meeting place. It is well understood that it is not only by discussion that the relevant values may emerge: study, silence and worship belong also to the process.

The church strives to make such communication possible, so that the exchange may transcend the mere piling up of goods and become a real communication, a mutual enrichment, a human relation. I see it in very concrete terms. Is not charity—real love—the passing on from those who have to those who have not? Has not the church to provide the necessary pipelines for the flow of knowledge, virtue, riches, comfort, health, joy? Not indeed to level down everything to an egalitarian stagnation, but to eliminate crying injustices and inhuman conditions.

How has the church to be reshaped in order to get the necessary mobility and flexibility? This is one of the basic problems of the practical reorganization which is now required. Perhaps the parish system has to be radically changed, and other groups have to emerge, based on other criteria. Much has already been written on this subject, so that we can leave it here. My aim is only to pin-point the problem and to state the issues.

2. COMMUNION—KOINONIA

One of the most invidious assumptions of modern Western culture is that man is an individual, a kind of atom or rather a monad (for not even physical atoms are individuals) with only extrinsic or accidental relations with others. Once this assumption is accepted, all efforts at perfection are going to tend towards self-sufficiency, identity in the sense of differentiation from others. It is often said that society is more than the mere sum of its individuals, and a city more than the agglomeration of its elements, but we usually overlook the simple reason for this: man himself is more than an individual.

The modern trend towards socialization and collectivization is a clear sign of this unavoidable truth and of a dynamism towards regaining a fuller personality in man transcending the individual. The negative character of more than one of these movements may be due to an exaggerated reaction against an opposite individualism, or to an undue emphasis on external bonds instead of recognizing the primordial reality which is not individuality but community.

In short, communication is not enough for a mature and complete human life; communion is further needed. I understand by communion not a kind of reunion (of individuals) or fellowship (among individuals), but the awareness of an inward and basic unity previous to the individualist diversification. Communion is not artificial, but rather a discovering the common roots and the primordial unity, and afterwards becoming aware that the differences are precisely different ways and manners of expressing that primary unity, like branches which really differ from one another but remain branches of the same tree.

One of the most important missions of the church is to provide the occasion for such an awareness.

Love is here the fundamental category. When love appears among two persons, for instance, it is not that they come together; rather they feel they belong together, and are really one which is split into two.

Celebration, liturgy, cult are here operative concepts. A tremendous revival could result from this point of view. The liturgy in its most general meaning is precisely the work—the action—of the people as people, the celebration of the community as such (and not of one individual whom the others follow). Liturgy is not the work of an individual or of many individuals for that matter, but the action of the people as people.

My point is now clear: the church is the place where such a communion is realized, re-enacted and strengthened. If a reading room or a lecture room, an agency for public relations, or a debating society can be urbanistic crystallizations of the church as *communication*, then a festival hall, a dining hall, a central plaza, the celebration of a certain feast and the like could be examples of the church as the ground for *communion*.

3. TRANCENDENCE—ECCLESIA

Man *has* indeed an individuality, he *is* also communion and community, but his richness is still greater, his dignity surpasses the so-called common good; for he is also an unfinished, i.e. a 'non-finite', an ever unfulfilled end, a transcendence. He is never satisfied, never achieved, and needs, so to speak, an open space and an open sky to give full expression to himself—to channel this ineffable longing of his being.

Not only are birth and death, suffering and decay, more or less transparent windows to this transcendence, but also joy, love, creativity and the like are signboards of this vertical dimension of man.

Here again, I would like to say that church is whatever provides an expression of this fact, an outlet for this desire, and that it is for the church to find appropriate ways of directing this human urge. Nothing is in the end going to satisfy the human heart, nothing is going to give a definitive answer to the human mind; and to avert idolatries, to avoid delusions, is one of the most specific tasks of the church.

Ecclesia means a congregation which is not yet congregated, a people which is still on the march, in the making, thus wrestling, struggling, worshipping and proceeding always farther and beyond. The heart of the *ecclesia* is always elsewhere, the tomb is empty, the Lord is not there, always, gone, ever risen.

A word of caution is here imperative for the church—of whatever religion. This vertical dimension of man has little to do with a sort of mysterious and dark side of things which claims to cover—and excuse—human ignorance. Only too often the church has mistaken phenomena which are 'mysterious'—because inexplicable for a certain time—for the real mystery. All sorts of obscurantism have from time to time grown under the wings of the church. And yet there is a real dimension of man which explains his thirsty condition and restless existence, unfulfillable by any measure.

The church cannot ignore this vertical, ever unfinished, infinite dimension of man, and it has to keep open such an attitude by not letting any answer be considered total, by not allowing any hope to crystallize too quickly or any ideal become an ideology. The church has a delicate function of disappointing man when he gets too enthusiastic about anything. It has to do this not by criticizing his noble efforts or by sneering self-complacently at his human attempts, but it has simply to keep open any formula so as to prevent any type of idolatry. 'If you happen to see the Buddha, then kill him', says an old Buddhist saying, which I would consider as one of the most sublime religious utterances ever made. 'It is good that I go away', said the Christ also, 'otherwise the Spirit will not come . . .' The function of the 'other shore' is to prevent us from falling asleep during our journey. All the structures of modern urbanism have to be provisional because they also, after a couple of decades or centuries perhaps, have to die, in order to rise again.

Mysticism, Silence, Prayer, Art, Mystery, Transcendence or whatever name is used for the matter, all are symbols of an ever greater and unachieved reality which is grasped only as we are incorporated in the very process.

How to provide for such a function? If our first point suggests that there are men with a certain vocation of passing on human communication—if our second point draws attention to man's community character, and thus leads us to consider the church as an embodiment of the community aspect of man—this third element reminds us of a transcendent ingredient in both man and the church. Certainly the church cannot manipulate the Holy Spirit, nor can we try to fit it somehow into urban planning. Yet there the space has to remain open and the time unfulfilled.

To sum up: after Incarnation, if we are going to take it seriously and thus not only to interpret it in an individualistic way—after Incarnation the City of God is the People of Man.

There is no longer a People of God over against peoples who are not God's. The City of God, the new Jerusalem, became also flesh, concrete, iron structures, streets, plazas, huts and palaces. It is up to us to discover this city, to develop it, to create it, to incarnate it with all that we have and that we are, we who live in the City of Man, which is also Son of God.

Bibliography

For those who would like to do some further reading about people and cities, here is a very short list selected from the many books that exist. Most of these should be easy to obtain.

Anderson, Nels *The Urban Community: A World Perspective*, New York, Holt, Reinhart and Winston (1959)

Frankenberg, R. *Communities in Britain: Social Life in Town and Country*, Penguin Books (1966)

Hall, Peter *The World Cities*, World University Library, Weidenfeld and Nicolson (1966)

Jacobs, Jane *The Death and Life of Great American Cities*, Cape (1962)

Konig, R. *The Community*, International Library of Sociology, Routledge (1968)

Little, K. *West African Urbanization: A Study of Voluntary Associations in Social Change*, Cambridge U.P. (1965)

Urban Development: Its Implications for Social Welfare; Proceedings of the Thirteenth International Conference of Social Work, Washington, Columbia U.P. (1966)

Wright, Frank Lloyd *The Living City*, New York, Horizon Press (1958)

The books about Christian ministry in urban areas are

fewer and less readily available. Here is a list of ten from which the reader can choose those obtainable locally.

Callahan, D. (Ed.)   The Secular City Debate, Collier-Macmillan (1967)

Cope, Gilbert (Ed.)   *Christian Ministry in New Towns,* University of Birmingham (1967)

Cox, Harvey   *The Secular City,* S.C.M. Press (1966)

Doxiadis, C. A. and Douglass, T. B.   *The New World of Urban Man,* Philadelphia, U.S.A., United Church Press (1965)

Fukuda, Robert (Ed.)   *God's People in Asian Industrial Society,* Kyoto, Doshisha University (1967)

Moore, Paul   *The Church Reclaims the City,* S.C.M. Press (1965)

Paradise, Scott   *Detroit Industrial Mission: A Personal Narration,* New York Harper and Row (1968)

Rossel, Jacques   *Mission in a Dynamic Society,* S.C.M. Press (1968)

Webber, George W.   *The   Congregation   in   Mission,* Nashville, U.S.A., Abingdon (1964)

Winter, Gibson   *The New Creation as Metropolis,* New York, Collier-Macmillan (1963)

PEOPLE AND CITIES

As Director of Studies for the 'People and Cities' conference at Coventry Cathedral in 1968, Canon Verney was responsible for bringing together representatives of 33 nations to share their experience of the modern city, and to search together for a new inspiration and a new positive vision of the city of the future. In this book his personal experience and the insights which he gained in the organizing of the conference are supplemented by the opinions of experts in urbanology.

Stephen Verney studied at Balliol, Oxford and Wescott House Theological College, Cambridge. During the war he served with the Friends' Ambulance Unit and later, as a member of the Intelligence Corps, worked with the Greek Resistance in Crete.

Before being appointed Canon Residentiary of Coventry Cathedral in 1964, he was vicar of a small country parish in Warwickshire, having previously been curate in Nottingham, first in Gedling and then on a housing estate.

He is currently organizing further-education courses for the clergy, to clarify the role and advance the work of the church in modern urban society.